✪ WEAPONS OF WAR
BATTLESHIPS AND AIRCRAFT CARRIERS
1900–PRESENT

CHARTWELL
BOOKS, INC.

CHARTWELL BOOKS, INC.
A division of BOOK SALES, INC.
276 Fifth Avenue Suite 206
New York, New York 10001
USA

Contributing authors: Chris Chant, Steve Crawford, Martin J. Dougherty, Ian Hogg,
Robert Jackson, Chris McNab, Michael Sharpe, Philip Trewhitt

ISBN 978-0-7858-2999-7

Printed in China

PICTURE CREDITS
Photographs:
Art-Tech/Aerospace: 10, 18, 19, 20 bottom, 21, 22
Art-Tech/MARS: 11, 13, 14/15
Cody Images: 6, 7, 8/9, 12, 16/17, 20 top, 23
U.S. Department of Defense: 24, 25

Ilustrations: © Amber Books, Art-Tech/Aerospace and Military Visualisations, Inc.

★ WEAPONS OF WAR
BATTLESHIPS AND AIRCRAFT CARRIERS
1900–PRESENT

CONTENTS

Introduction

Capital ships

At the turn of the 20th century, the battleship was still king, but, by the 1940s, the aircraft carrier had changed that.

In any country's navy, the battleship and aircraft carrier are not just its biggest and most powerful vessels, they are also a symbol of that nation's maritime strength, its ambition, and its wealth. The ships described and illustrated in this book cover a huge variety of types and sizes of vessel, from coastal defence ships of the nineteenth century such as the Arminius of Prussia, to

the vast nuclear-powered aircraft carriers like USS Enterprise of today's US Navy.

All the ships illustrated in this book were all built to fight. That is their ultimate purpose, and the technical innovations which have attempted to give one ship a fighting edge over another has always been the driving force behind their design and construction. What began in the

MINAS GERAIS: see page 132–133

WEAPONS OF WAR

1850s with steam engines in the hulls of wooden three-deckers, such as the French *Bretagne*, created within 40 years the big-gun battleship, epitomized by Japan's armoured giant *Yamato* of World War II; the main gun turrets of which would weigh more than the whole of *Bretagne* under full sail. Ships such as the *Yamato* are the archetypal 'big' warship, but smaller vessels of previous centuries are also classified as capital ships. The reader should be aware that the definition of a battleship is a large, heavily armed armoured vessel armed with large-calibre guns. Thus, the *Ark Royal* of 400 years ago was one of Queen Elizabeth I's battleships, just as the *Stonewall* was for the Confederacy 200 years later. The

logical progression of this development is quite clear in the history of many of the ships featured in this book. The *Agincourt* of 1862, for example, had her guns set in a broadside exactly the same as the *Ark Royal* of 300 years before. She had a steam engine, but still relied on her sails at sea for economical wind power. Her armour was made up of iron plates backed onto a greater thickness of wood, making her literally an 'ironclad'. Like many of her time, however, she was already being fitted with rifled, breech-loading guns, which were more accurate and had a longer range than the old smoothbore muzzle-loading weapons. Her guns would also be firing explosive shells. Perfected by the French in the 1840s, they

DREADNOUGHT: see page 65

AGINCOURT: see page 28–29

WEAPONS OF WAR

IRON DUKE: see page 116

WEAPONS OF WAR

WARSPITE: see page 170

Launched in 1860, the Royal Navy's *Warrior* was the first warship to have an iron hull.

had proved their destructiveness in 1853, during the Battle of Sinope between the Russians and Turks.

So guns were becoming more effective and munitions more destructive, and the answer to that threat lay in more defensive armour. The French *Gloire* of 1859 boasted a wide wrought iron belt running from below the waterline to her upper deck, backed by up to 650mm (25.6in) of wooden hull. However, wood was becoming obsolete. *Warrior*, launched the following year for the Royal Navy, was the first ship to have an iron hull. She carried four 70-pounder and ten 110-pounder guns, which outclassed *Gloire* and made *Warrior* the most powerful warship in the world. But not for long.

A Royal Navy officer called Cowper Coles wrote to the Admiralty in 1861, claiming he

could disable and capture *Warrior* in an hour using a ship of his own design which cost half as much as *Warrior* to build, and which employed half the men. His secret was the gun turret. The Lords of the Admiralty accepted Cowper Coles' challenge. The *Prince Albert* was launched in 1864 and proved the potential of the gun turret, which could after all bring guns to bear on a target far faster than any ship with guns ranged along the hull. However, she could never match *Warrior* as a sea-going vessel, being too lightly rigged with sail, and her steam engine was not powerful enough for the weight of the armoured hull and the armoured turrets, each of which weighed 112 tonnes (111 tons) and had to be worked by hand.

Refusing to be discouraged, Cowper Coles went on to try and prove the viability of a sea-going turreted warship when he built *Captain* in 1869. She was fully rigged and, to prevent the masts getting in the way, the turrets were placed very low to the water. Unfortunately all this made her unseaworthy, and she capsized in a storm during her trials, taking most of the crew and Cowper Coles with her.

THE TRIUMPH OF TURRETED WARSHIPS

By the early 1870s, armoured warships with turrets had proved themselves in combat. During the American Civil War in 1862, *Monitor* of the US Navy had beaten the CSS *Virginia* in the first gun duel between completely armoured steam-driven vessels. But the combat was in shallow coastal waters and *Monitor* was later to suffer the same fate as *Captain*; she tried to take to the open sea and foundered in heavy weather. It seemed as if such designs would always be restricted to coastal defence and shallow waters.

The drawbacks to armour and steam, however, did not curb the ambitions of either designers, ship builders or navies. It was clear that the advantages of a fighting ship with steam power, armour plate and big guns were too great to be ignored for the sake of the practical problems involved in getting the right balance of all three. A ship needed enough armour to defend itself against the guns of an enemy vessel, a hull big enough to house the engines necessary to propel that weight at sufficient speed, and guns big enough to match, if not outrange, any others. It was a technical conundrum which the greatest technical minds of the age tried to solve, and which resulted in the 1870s and 1880s in huge variety of ship designs.

GRAF SPEE: see page 96

WEAPONS OF WAR

HOOD: see page 106

The position of guns in these vessels posed a special problem, particularly until the mid-1870s, when guns and turrets had to be positioned around the full rig of sails and masts most capital ships still carried. The guns needed to be sufficiently protected, but had to be high enough off the waterline to avoid being flooded and taking the ship down. Some vessels, such as the Turkish *Lufi Djelil*, had hinged bulwarks that could be lowered to allow their turrets clear fields of fire, while others, such as *Caimen* of France, had guns placed in raised armoured redoubts called barbettes. Another solution, seen in France's massive battleship Dévastation, was to have the main armament amidships inside a central battery.

THE RAM BOW

One feature, however, which characterized most ocean-going capital ships of the period was the ram bow. Designers were greatly influenced by the ramming and sinking of the Italian battleship *Re d'Italia* at the Battle of Lissa in 1866. Despite the fact that the biggest naval guns now had a range of over 27km (15nm), many saw the fate of the *Re d'Italia* as proof that ramming was a viable naval tactic and a practical use for an iron hull. For the next 30 years, warships would

BISMARCK: see page 49

WEAPONS OF WAR

feature the chisel-like ram bow, and some, such as the Confederate commerce raider *Stonewall*, would be built specifically as rams.

However, this period of experimental warship design could go on indefinitely. A fleet could not be sent to sea if its every vessel was of a different type, with different sailing characteristics, carrying a different calibre gun. In 1889, the British Admiralty called a halt and ordered the building of an entirely new fleet of 70 ships, including eight standard first-class battleships. The resulting capital class vessel of this fleet was the *Royal Sovereign* of 1892. Her hull and guns were of steel, she was protected by armour plate up to 450mm (17.7in) thick and carried guns of 343mm (13.5in) calibre. Even though she displaced nearly 16,000 tonnes (15,744 tons), she could still make 16 knots.

BIG-GUN BATTLESHIP

The era of the big-gun battleship had arrived. But the economic cost was enormous. Naval expenditure in Britain rose by 290 per cent during the 1890s and, by the end of the decade, the cost of each new Royal Navy battleship was approaching £1.5 million. Not that such considerations caused any slow-down in warship construction. The world had embarked on its first great arms race, and every industrialized country – and many, such as Brazil, who weren't – saw the possession of a navy, and particularly battleships, as a mark of their power and self-esteem. The competitive spirit in this race was particularly strong in the new world powers such as Imperial Germany and the United States, who both spent twice as

RICHELIEU: see page 155

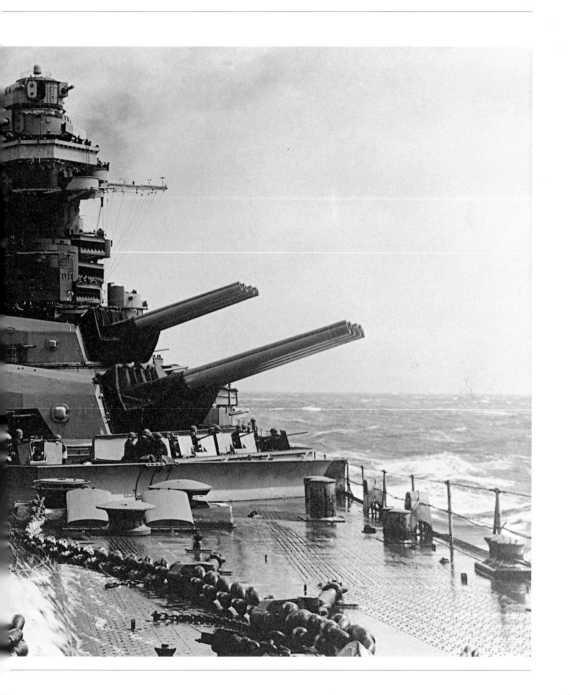

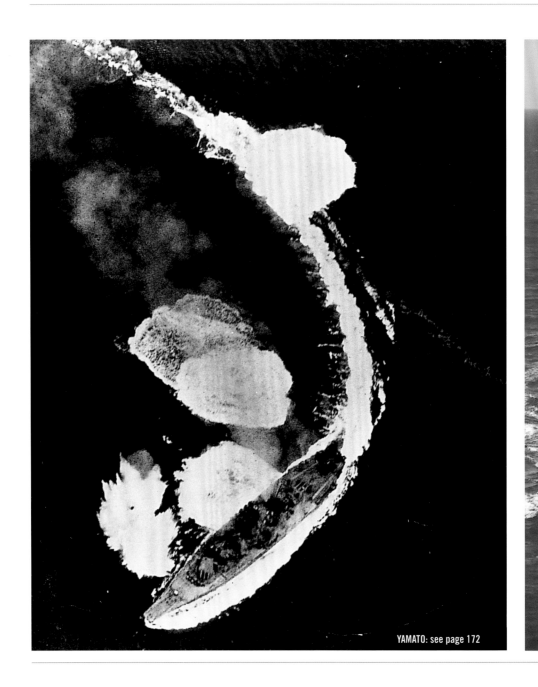

YAMATO: see page 172

IOWA: see page 115

much as the British on their navies in an effort to catch up.

But the British had begun this arms race, to all intents and purposes, and were not going to risk losing their naval supremacy. Quality was what was going to keep the Royal Navy ahead, even though official policy (known as the Two Power Standard) stated that they maintain a navy bigger than any other two of the largest navies in the world combined. In 1906, they launched HMS *Dreadnought*, a ship which combined every single technical advance to date, from new steam turbine engines to electrically controlled gun turrets. *Dreadnought* made obsolete every other battleship in the world, including those in her own navy, and gave her name to an entirely new class of warship.

As with many of the record-breaking vessels of the past, however, *Dreadnought's* time as the world's number one did not last very long. By 1908 the Royal Navy was building so-called 'superdreadnoughts', ships such as *Iron Duke*, which were over 8128 tonnes (8000 tons) heavier.

The future of the capital ship seemed to lie in bigger and bigger battleships carrying guns of ever-increasing size. But in the years just prior to World War I, questions were being asked as to the battleship's future. While the sheer technical achievement in building them was celebrated, many – including senior Royal Navy officers – were wondering exactly how useful in battle these huge floating gun batteries would be. Countries such as Germany were ceding the battleship contest and were beginning to develop other warship types such as the battle cruiser, vessels designed for fast commerce raiding rather than naval battles,

ARK ROYAL: see page 36

AKAGI: see page 31

WEAPONS OF WAR

ENTERPRISE: see page 74

ESSEX: see page 77

The aircraft was recognized as a potential weapon in naval warfare as far back as 1894.

which would find ultimate expression in the great German raiders of World War II, such as *Scharnhorst* and *Bismarck*. More ominously, Germany was also investing in a fleet of torpedo-carrying submarines.

THE FIRST AIRCRAFT CARRIERS

It was to be the aircraft, though, which would ultimately make the battleship redundant. Recognized as a potential weapon in naval warfare as far back as 1894, it was the Americans who began work

trying to fly an aircraft off a warship when, in January 1911, Lieutenant Theodore G. Ellyson landed a biplane on the converted deck of the cruiser Pennsylvania.

Aircraft were used for reconnaissance and target-spotting during World War I, but their offensive capabilities were not fully explored until the 1920s. Pioneers such as Brigadier-General 'Billy' Mitchell in the United States proved that ships could be destroyed by bombardment from the air. In trials in 1921, his aircraft even sunk the

22

HERMES: see page 105

FOCH (R99): see page 80

Today, the US Navy's carrier battle group is the most potent expression of naval power in the world.

ex-German dreadnought *Ostfriedland*, though it took two days of attacks and 19 bomb hits to complete the job. However, the United States Navy was convinced and, in 1922, its first aircraft carrier, *Langley*, was launched. Four years later, plans for specially designed carrier-based aircraft were on the drawing board.

There was a new offensive weapon in the naval arsenal, but throughout the 1920s and 1930s traditionalists held firm that any future naval warfare would be decided by battleships, despite the fact that they were restricted by international disarmament

treaties in 1921 and 1930, which effectively stopped battleship construction for 10 years and restricted gross tonnage when building started again.

At the beginning of World War II, battleships such as *Haruna* of Japan and the Royal Navy's HMS *Nelson* still represented the most powerful war machines made by man. But by 1942, the type had been completely eclipsed by the practicalities of a new kind of warfare, and faith in the power of the battleship had vanished forever. Air raids by torpedo planes on Taranto and Pearl Harbor, the sinking of *Repulse* and

GEORGE WASHINGTON: see page 88

Prince of Wales off Malaya, the attacks on British battleships *Barham, Warspite, Queen Elizabeth* and *Valiant* in the Mediterranean, all proved that a battleship could not exist without control of the air space above it. And while there were a few successes for the old style gunnery warfare – the sinking of *Haruna* by USS *Washington* off Guadalcanal, for example – it was clear that the best practical use for a battleship was in shore bombardment or as a gun platform for scores of anti-aircraft guns. The age of the aircraft carrier as a capital ship, had arrived.

CARRIER POWER TODAY

Since the end of World War II, the carrier has remained as the most powerful type of naval vessel, and the ultimate expression of national force projection. The US Navy's carrier battle group represents the apogee of the aircraft carrier. A carrier battle group consists of one or two carriers, each capable of deploying an air wing (which on average contains nine squadrons of aircraft, ranging from F/A-18 and F-14 fighters to SH-60 helicopters). And yet they require substantial naval assets to protect them from both air and submarine attack: guided-missile cruisers, guided-missile destroyers, anti-submarine warfare destroyers, anti-submarine warfare frigates and even one or two nuclear submarines; proof that the capital ship, no matter how powerful, is always vulnerable.

Admiral Graf Spee

Limited by the 1919 Treaty of Versailles to a maximum displacement of 10,200 tonnes (10,039 tons), Germany produced the cleverly designed 'pocket' battleship. Great savings were achieved by using electric welding and light alloys in the hull. *Admiral Graf Spee*, with her two sister ships, *Deutschland* and *Admiral Scheer*, were intended primarily as commerce-raiders. The ship was scuttled off Montevideo, Uruguay, after engaging three British cruisers: *Exeter*, *Ajax* and *Achilles*, in the Battle of the River Plate in December 1939. This ship was officially classified as being an 'armoured ship' by the Germans, though it was popularly referred to as being a 'pocket' battleship, a title which stuck. In actual fact neither term is strictly correct, for she was in reality an armoured cruiser of an exceptionally powerful type.

SPECIFICATIONS

COUNTRY OF ORIGIN: Germany
CREW: 926
WEIGHT: 10,160 tonnes (10,000 tons)
DIMENSIONS: 186m x 20.6m x 7.2m (610ft 3in x 67ft 7in x 23ft 7in)
RANGE: 37,040km (20,000nm) at 15 knots
ARMOUR: 76mm (3in) belt, 140–76mm (5.5–3in) on turrets, 38mm (1.5in) on deck
ARMAMENT: 6 x 279mm (11in), 8 x 150mm (6in) guns
POWERPLANT: eight sets of MAN diesels, two shafts
PERFORMANCE: 26 knots

Admiral Kuznetsov

The 'Kiev' class could never be considered true aircraft carriers. From the 1960s onwards, the rapidly expanding Soviet Navy began to see its lack of such a vessel to be a handicap. In the early 1980s, two projects began to make serious progress, one of which became the *Admiral Kuznetsov*. Although superficially similar to American carriers, the Soviet aircraft carrier was always intended to be subordinate to missile submarines operating in their 'bastions' in the Arctic. It is capable of engaging surface, subsurface and airborne targets. The flight deck area is 14,700m² (158,235ft²) and aircraft take-off is assisted by a bow ski-jump angled at 12 degrees in lieu of steam catapults. The ship was designed to operate Su-27K, MiG-29K and Yak-41 (and later the heavier and more capable Yak-43) supersonic STOVL fighters. In early April 2010, it was announced that by the end of 2012 the ship would enter Severodvinsk Sevmash shipyard for a major refit.

SPECIFICATIONS

COUNTRY OF ORIGIN: Russia
CREW: 2626, including 626 air personnel and 40 flag staff
WEIGHT: 46,600 tonnes (45,864 tons) standard; 59,400 tonnes (58,462 tons) fully loaded
DIMENSIONS: 304.5m x 67m x 11m (999ft x 219ft 10in x 36ft 1in) (hangar deck 183m/600ft)
RANGE: 7130km (3850nm) at 32 knots
ARMOUR: unknown
ARMAMENT: 12-cell VLS for P-700 Granit (SS-N-19 'Shipwreck') SSMs, 24 x eight-round Kinshal (SA-N-9 'Gauntlet') vertical SAM launchers with 192 missiles, 8 x combined gun/missile close air defence systems with 8 x twin 30mm (1.18in) (Gatling guns and Klinok (SA-N-11 'Grison') missiles, 2 x RPK-5 (UDAV-1) ASW rocket systems with 60 rockets
POWERPLANT: steam turbines, eight turbo-pressurized boilers, four shafts, 149,140kW (200,000hp)
PERFORMANCE: 32 knots

Agincourt

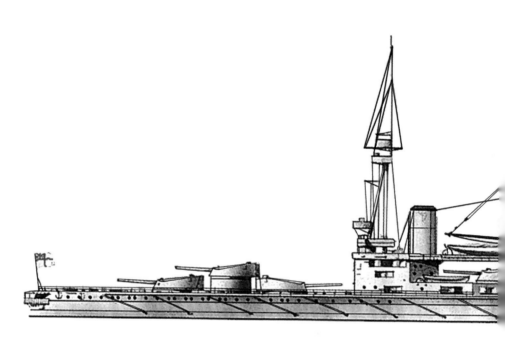

Originally ordered in Britain by the Brazilian Government and named *Rio de Janiero* when she launched in 1913, the Brazilians found they could not afford her. She was sold on to Turkey as *Sultan Osman I*, but never delivered. Completed in August 1914, she was appropriated by the Royal Navy for war service and renamed *Agincourt*. In design she had many unusual features, not least her length and main armament of 14 304mm (12in) guns on seven twin turrets. However, this huge amount of weight weakened her hull, which was in any case woefully underprotected. She was nevertheless known in her time as a good sea boat. Her tripod main mast was reduced to a pole in 1917 and later removed. After World War I, *Agincourt* was unsuccessfully offered for sale back to Brazil, and sold for scrap in the 1920s.

SPECIFICATIONS

COUNTRY OF ORIGIN: United Kingdom
CREW: 1270
WEIGHT: 27,940 tonnes (27,500 tons)
DIMENSIONS: 204.7m x 27.1m x 8.2m (671ft 6in x 89ft x 27ft)
RANGE: 8100km (4500nm) at 12 knots
ARMOUR: 229–102mm (9–4in) belt, 152mm (6in) on bulkheads
ARMAMENT: 14 x 304mm (12in), 20 x 152mm (6in), 10 x 76mm (3in) guns
POWERPLANT: four-shaft geared turbines
PERFORMANCE: 22 knots

Agamemnon

Agamemnon was one of the Lord Nelson class and the last of Britain's pre-dreadnoughts. Laid down in 1904, her construction coincided with that of HMS *Dreadnought*. As a result, *Agamemnon*'s completion was delayed until 1908, by which time *Dreadnought* had made history and the Lord Nelson class was launched into virtual obsolescence. Characterized by their large secondary armament, which differed of course from the all big-gun dreadnoughts, the class was known at the time for having a rather French look to its design, with a high superstructure and low unequal-sized funnels. *Agamemnon* served in the eastern Mediterranean during World War I, and saw action in the Dardenelles. During these operations she was hit over 60 times and, on 15 May 1916, her gunners shot down Zeppelin L85 at Salonika.

SPECIFICATIONS

COUNTRY OF ORIGIN: United Kingdom
CREW: 810
WEIGHT: 16,347 tonnes (16,090 tons)
DIMENSIONS: 124m x 135m x 24m (406ft 10in x 44ft 6in x 79ft 6in)
RANGE: 17,000km (9180nm) at 10 knots
ARMOUR: 304–203mm (12–8in) belt, 178–304mm (7.11in) on citadel and turrets
ARMAMENT: 4 x 304mm (12in), 10 x 234mm (9.2in), 24 x 12-pounder guns, 5 x torpedo tubes
POWERPLANT: twin-shaft four cylinder engine
PERFORMANCE: 18 knots

Akagi

Akagi was designed as a 41,820 tonne (41,161 ton) battlecruiser, but, while still on the stocks, the Washington Naval Treaty of 1922 (whereby Japan was forced to restrict her naval programme) caused the design to be altered. Built to dispatch up to 60 aircraft, she was modified to carry heavier aircraft and more light guns. As converted, she had three flight decks forward, no island and two funnels on the starboard side, one pointing up, the other out and down. During reconstruction (1935–38) the two lower flight decks forward were removed and the top flight deck extended forward to the bow. An island was added on the port side. Akagi led the Japanese carrier assault on Pearl Harbor on 7 December 1941, but was destroyed seven months later by bombs dropped by US Navy dive-bombers at the decisive Battle of Midway.

SPECIFICATIONS

COUNTRY OF ORIGIN: Japan
CREW: 2000
WEIGHT: 29,580 tonnes (29,114 tons)
DIMENSIONS: 249m x 30.5m x 8.1m (816ft 11in x 100ft 1in x 26ft 7in)
RANGE: 14,800km (8000nm) at 14 knots
ARMOUR: 152mm (6in) belt
ARMAMENT: 10 x 203mm (8in), 12 x 119mm (4.7in) guns, 91 x aircraft
POWERPLANT: four-shaft turbines
PERFORMANCE: 32.5 knots

Alberto da Giussano

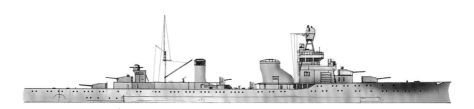

One of a class of four units built to counter the powerful French Lion class destroyers, *Alberto da Giussano* represented an extremely efficient class of ship. Lightly armoured, she was one of the fastest destroyers in the world at the time of her launch; one of her class achieved a speed of 42 knots during trials and maintained a steady 40 knots for eight hours. Classified as a light cruiser before the outbreak of World War II, the *da Giussano* became part of the Italian Navy's 4th Division at Italy's entry into the war in June 1940, and undertook many minelaying operations. Together with a sister ship, *Alberico da Barbiano*, she was sunk by the British destroyers *Legion* and *Maori* on 13 December 1941, 900 lives being lost in the two ships.

SPECIFICATIONS

COUNTRY OF ORIGIN: Denmark
CREW: 100
WEIGHT: 6300 tonnes (6200 tons) fully loaded
DIMENSIONS: 137m x 19.5m x 6.3m (450ft x 64ft x 20ft 8in)
RANGE: 7037km (3800nm)
ARMOUR:
ARMAMENT: 1 x Mk 54 127mm (5in) gun; 2 x 35mm (1.38in) guns; 8 or 16 x RGM-84 Harpoon anti-ship missiles; 36 x VLS cells for ESSM; plus anti-submarine torpedoes, mines and additional light automatic weapons and/or surface-to-air missiles. Two helicopters
POWERPLANT: 2 x MTU 8000 M/70 Diesel (8.31MW; 11,139hp each)
PERFORMANCE: up to 40 knots

America

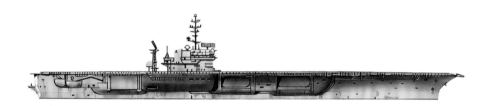

The Kitty Hawk class were the first aircraft carriers not to carry conventional guns. Intended to be larger and improved versions of the earlier Forrestal class, *Kitty Hawk* (CV 63) and *Constellation* (CV 64) were the first two built. The third, *America* (CV 66), was launched in 1964, and incorporated further improvements based on operational experience. Her dimensions are slightly different to those of her sisters, with a narrower smokestack. *America* was the first carrier to be equipped with an integrated Combat Information Centre (CIC) and is also fitted with a bow-mounted sonar. A fourth ship, *John F. Kennedy* (CV 67), was built after the US Congress refused to sanction a nuclear-powered vessel in 1964. Policy has since changed, and all large US carriers since then have used nuclear propulsion, leaving *America* and her sisters as the largest conventionally driven vessels in service.

SPECIFICATIONS

COUNTRY OF ORIGIN United States
CREW: 3306, or 1379 with air group
WEIGHT: 81,090 tonnes (79,813 tons) fully loaded
DIMENSIONS: 324m x 77m x 10.7m (1063ft x 252ft 7in x 35ft 1in)
RANGE: 21,600km (12,000nm) at 12 knots
ARMOUR: belt 51mm (2in)
ARMAMENT: 3 x Mark 29 launchers for NATO Sea Sparrow SAMs, 3 x 20mm (0.79in) Phalanx CIWS (Close-in Weapons System), 90 x aircraft
POWERPLANT: four-shaft geared turbines
PERFORMANCE: 33 knots

Andrea Doria

L aid down in 1912, and launched four years later in 1916, *Andrea Doria*, and her sister ship *Caio Duilio*, both underwent a very rigorous reconstruction programme from 1937 to 1940. *Andrea Doria*'s top speed was increased from 21.5 to 27 knots; in addition, she was given improved armour on her turrets and engine rooms. During World War I, she operated in the southern Adriatic, and subsequently in 1919 she operated in the Black Sea, supporting the Allied Intervention Force operating in South Russia on the loyalist side during the civil war. During World War II, *Andrea Doria* took part in convoy battles and in some notable actions, including the First Battle of Sirte. She was placed on the Reserve in 1942, and in the following year she surrendered to the British at Malta. Both ships remained in service until 1958.

SPECIFICATIONS

COUNTRY OF ORIGIN: Italy
CREW: 1198
WEIGHT: 26,115 tonnes (25,704 tons)
DIMENSIONS: 176m x 28m x 8.8m (577ft 5in x 91ft 10in x 28ft 10in)
RANGE: 8784km (4800nm) at 10 knots (before reconstruction)
ARMOUR: 229mm (9in) belt, 229mm (9in) turrets, 127mm (5in) on guns
ARMAMENT: 13 x 304mm (12in), 16 x 152mm (6in) guns
POWERPLANT: twin-shaft geared turbines
PERFORMANCE: 26 knots

Arizona

Arizona, like her sister ship *Pennsylvania*, was an improved and enlarged version of the Nevada class, her main armament being housed in four triple turrets. Launched in 1915, and completed the following year, *Arizona* did not see any action during World War I. In 1941, she sailed to the Pacific to join the US fleet based at Pearl Harbor. On the morning of 7 December, the Japanese launched an air attack without warning. One of the first ships hit was the *Arizona*. A bomb is believed to have struck one of her forward turrets, which detonated the magazine beneath. The ship blew up, taking over a thousand members of her crew with her. *Arizona* was one of four US battleships sunk at Pearl Harbor; a fifth was beached and three more were damaged. Today her remains still lie in the shallow waters of the harbour where she is preserved as a war grave.

SPECIFICATIONS

COUNTRY OF ORIGIN United States
CREW: 1117
WEIGHT: 32,045 tonnes (32,567 tons)
DIMENSIONS: 185.4m x 29.6m x 8.8m (608ft 3in x 97ft 1in x 28ft 10in)
RANGE: 14,400km (8000nm) at 10 knots
ARMOUR: 343–203mm (13.5–8in) belt, 450–229mm (18in–9in) on turrets
ARMAMENT: 12 x 356mm (14in), 22 x 127mm (5in) guns
POWERPLANT: four-shaft geared turbines
PERFORMANCE: 21 knots

Ark Royal

Ark Royal was the first large purpose-built aircraft carrier to be constructed for the Royal Navy, with a long flight deck some 18m (60ft) above the deep water load line. The aircraft carrier's full complement was 60 aircraft, although she never actually carried this many, as such a load would have reduced her fighting capability. During her war operations, Ark Royal took part in the Norwegian campaign of 1940 and was subsequently transferred to the Mediterranean Theatre, where she joined 'Force H' at Gibraltar. In May 1941, one of her Swordfish aircraft torpedoed the German battleship Bismarck, destroying the warship's steering gear, an act that led to Bismarck being sunk some hours later by the British Fleet. In November 1941, Ark Royal was torpedoed by the German submarine U81 and capsized after 14 hours.

SPECIFICATIONS
COUNTRY OF ORIGIN United Kingdom
CREW: 1580
WEIGHT: 28,164 tonnes (27,720 tons)
DIMENSIONS: 243.8m x 28.9m x 8.5m (800ft x 94ft 9in x 27ft 9in)
RANGE: 14,119km (7620nm) at 20 knots
ARMOUR: 114mm (4.5in) belt, 76mm (3in) bulkheads
ARMAMENT: 16 x 114mm (4.5in) guns, 60 x aircraft
POWERPLANT: triple-shaft geared turbines
PERFORMANCE: 31 knots

Armando Diaz

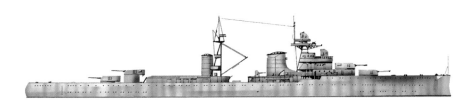

Armando Diaz and her sister ship
Luigi Cadorna were part of the Italian
Navy's building programme of between
1929 and 1930, and were originally
classified as light cruisers. They bore
a strong resemblance to the previous
group of fast cruisers, but they had more
internal space, which in turn permitted
reduced upperworks and a smaller bridge.
These improvements helped to enhance
the vessels' stability in heavy seas. Both
ships had a seaplane catapult on the rear
superstructure. They could carry up to
138 mines, depending on the type. Both
ships, reclassified as destroyers, operated
extensively in the Mediterranean during
World War II, but Armando Diaz was
sunk in February 1941 when the British
submarine HMS Upright torpedoed her
while she was in the process of escorting
a convoy.

SPECIFICATIONS
COUNTRY OF ORIGIN Italy
CREW: 220
WEIGHT: 5406 tonnes (5321 tons)
DIMENSIONS: 169.3m x 15.5m x 5.5m (555ft 6in x
50ft 10in x 18ft 1in)
RANGE: 5185km (2800nm)
ARMOUR: 114mm (4.5in) belt, 76mm (3in) bulkheads
ARMAMENT: 8 x 152mm (6in) guns
POWERPLANT: twin-shaft geared turbines
PERFORMANCE: 36.5 knots

Attu

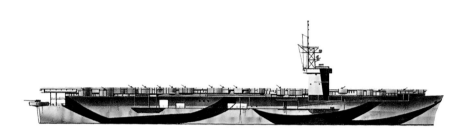

In 1942, shipbuilder Henry J. Kaiser was employed in the mass production of cargo vessels to replace those that had been lost in action. It was decided at that time to complete 50 of the unfinished hulls as escort carriers. The resultant vessel was named *Attu* (CVE 102). Her 49 sister ships (of the Casablanca class) were all completed within a single year. The Casablanca class carried an air group of nine bombers, nine torpedo-bombers and nine fighters. They were the first vessels of their kind to be built as escort carriers from the keel up. All of the Casablanca class went on to serve in the Pacific, with the exception of *Guadalcanal* and *Kasaan Bay*, both of which saw service in the Atlantic. In 1947, *Attu* was converted for mercantile use and renamed *Gay*. She was subsequently scrapped at Baltimore in 1949.

SPECIFICATIONS

COUNTRY OF ORIGIN United States
CREW: 860
WEIGHT: 11,076 tonnes (10,902 tons)
DIMENSIONS: 156.1m x 32.9m x 6.3m (512ft 3in x 108ft x 20ft 9in)
RANGE: 18,360km (10,200nm) at 10 knots
ARMOUR: flight deck unarmoured
ARMAMENT: 1 x 127mm (5in), 38 x 40mm (1.5in) guns, 27 x aircraft
POWERPLANT: twin-screw reciprocating engines
PERFORMANCE: 15 knots

Audacious

Built in answer to the growing strength and ambition of the German Navy, *Audacious*, one of the King George V class, was part of the 1911 British battleship expansion programme. She carried the foremast before the funnels, giving better vision to fire control when underway, a standard arrangement on all subsequent dreadnoughts. While on patrol in October 1914, *Audacious* struck a mine off Ireland and all attempts to tow her to safety failed. She was the first major British warship lost in World War I. Of the other two vessels in her class, *King George V* served as a gunnery training ship after World War I, and was broken up in 1926, and *Centurion* went on to see service in World War II as a floating AA battery in the Mediterranean. *Audacious* was sunk off Normandy in June 1944 to form part of an artificial harbour.

SPECIFICATIONS

COUNTRY OF ORIGIN United Kingdom
CREW: 782
WEIGHT: 26,111 tonnes (25,700 tons)
DIMENSIONS: 182.1m x 27.1m x 8.7m (597ft 6in x 89ft x 28ft 6in)
RANGE: 12,114km (6730nm) at 10 knots
ARMOUR: 305–203mm (12.8–7.9in) main belt with 280mm (11in) on turrets
ARMAMENT: 10 x 342mm (13.5in), 16 x 102mm (4in) guns
POWERPLANT: four-shaft geared turbines
PERFORMANCE: 21 knots

Australia

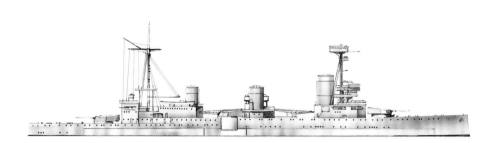

Australia was a new type of cruiser. Improvements in speed had been achieved by reducing armour protection, and by reducing the main guns by two. In addition, the middle group of turrets, placed in échelon, had a greater field of fire. Australia was built on the Clyde in 1913 and, after completion, she sailed to the Pacific to become the flagship of the Royal Australian Navy. She returned to Britain mid-way through World War I, but was unable to take part in the Battle of Jutland as the result of a collision with the battlecruiser New Zealand in fog. In December 1916, Australia was damaged in another collision, this time with the battlecruiser Repulse. Australia was decommissioned in December 1921, and was subsequently used as a target ship, until she was sunk off Sydney in April 1924.

SPECIFICATIONS

COUNTRY OF ORIGIN Australia
CREW: 800
WEIGHT: 21,640 tonnes (21,300 tons)
DIMENSIONS: 180m x 24.3m x 9m (590ft 7in x 79ft 9in x 29ft 6in)
RANGE: 11,394km (6330nm) at 10 knots
ARMOUR: 152mm (6in) belt
ARMAMENT: 8 x 304mm (12in) guns
POWERPLANT: four-screw geared turbines
PERFORMANCE: 26.9 knots

Baden

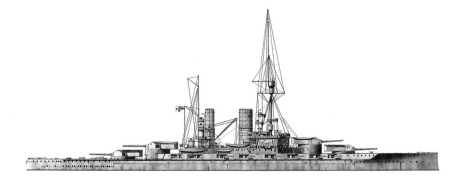

Baden and her sister, *Bayern,* were completed in 1916. In contrast to earlier classes in the Imperial German Navy, such as the *König,* their main armament: was increased from 304mm (12in) to 380mm (15in). This was to match the guns rumoured to be carried on the new British Queen Elizabeth class. Unusually for a battleship of the period, *Baden* was coal-fired, since wartime fuel oil supplies in Germany were too unpredictable. Commissioned too late to have much impact on World War I, *Baden* was Fleet Flagship from October 1916, replacing *Friedrich der Grosse,* and surrendered in 1918. She was not scheduled to be surrendered, but was substituted for the incomplete *Mackensen.* She was unsuccessfully scuttled at Scapa Flow in 1919 and, after being salvaged by the Royal Navy, was used as a gunnery target, then sunk.

SPECIFICATIONS

COUNTRY OF ORIGIN: Germany
CREW: 1271
WEIGHT: 32,197 tonnes (31,690 tons) deep load
DIMENSIONS: 179.8m x 30m x 8.43m (589ft 10in x 98ft 5in x 27ft 8in)
RANGE: 9000km (5000nm) at 10 knots
ARMOUR: 356–120mm (14–4.7in) belt, 304–140mm (12–5.5in) bulkheads, 356–102mm (14–4in) turrets
ARMAMENT: 8 x 380mm (15in), 16 x 150mm (5.9in) guns
POWERPLANT: three-shaft turbines
PERFORMANCE: 22 knots

Barham

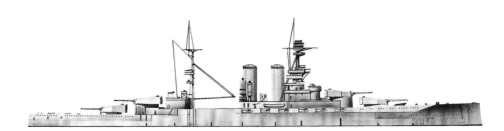

Barham and her three sisters were designed to compete with new battleships – with 355mm (14in) guns – being designed by Germany, Japan and the US. The class was equipped with newly designed 380mm (15in) guns, which proved more accurate than the previous 343mm (13.5in) guns, and also carried a much bigger bursting charge. *Barham* was badly damaged at Jutland in 1916. All ships in the class underwent modernization in the early 1930s. *Barham* was sunk with heavy loss of life off Sollum in the Mediterranean by U331 on 25 November 1941. The other ships in Barham's class were *Malaya*, *Queen Elizabeth*, *Valiant* and *Warspite*. After extensive war service, they were broken up in 1947–48. *Valiant* and *Queen Elizabeth* were badly damaged in a daring attack by Italian frogmen in Alexandria harbour in 1941.

SPECIFICATIONS

COUNTRY OF ORIGIN United Kingdom
CREW: 951
WEIGHT: 32,004 tonnes (31,500 tons)
DIMENSIONS: 196m x 27.6m x 8.8m (643ft x 90ft 6in x 29ft)
RANGE: 26,100km (14,500nm) at 10 knots
ARMOUR: 330–152mm (13–6in) belt, 330mm (15in) turrets
ARMAMENT: 8 x 381mm (15in), 14 x 152mm (6in) guns
POWERPLANT: four-shaft turbines
PERFORMANCE: 24 knots

Béarn

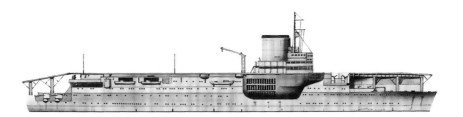

The aircraft carrier *Béarn* was converted from the incompleted hull of a Normandie class battleship, and her original turbine propulsion was replaced by the combined system that was designed for that vessel. In October 1939, she formed a key element of a hunting group (Force L) based on Brest, which, together with other British and French naval forces, was engaged in the search for the German pocket battleship *Admiral Graf Spee*. Apart from that, *Béarn* was not used as a frontline carrier in World War II because of her low speed, but she gave valuable service as an aircraft ferry. After the fall of France in 1940, *Béarn* was captured and held at Martinique to prevent her return to France. After the war she served off Indo-China (Vietnam) during France's conflict there. She was scrapped in 1949.

SPECIFICATIONS

COUNTRY OF ORIGIN France
CREW: 875
WEIGHT: 28,854 tonnes (28,400 tons)
DIMENSIONS: 182.5m x 27m x 9m (599ft x 88ft 11in x 30ft 6in)
RANGE: 14,824km (6000nm) at 10 knots
ARMOUR: 94mm (3.75in) belt, 25mm (1in) flight deck
ARMAMENT: 8 x 152mm (6in) guns, 40 x aircraft
POWERPLANT: four-screw geared turbines, triple-expansion engines
PERFORMANCE: 21.5 knots

Bellerophon

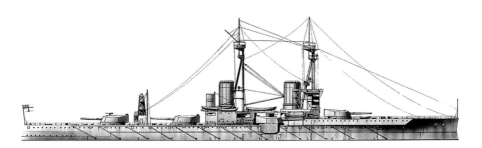

Launched in 1907, *Bellerophon* and her sisters *Temeraire* and *Superb* closely followed the dimensions of HMS *Dreadnought*, though their torpedo defences were increased with improvements to bulkhead armour and secondary armament. When completed in 1909, the Bellerophon class also had masts in front of funnels. This avoided the smoke problems to the command top encountered on *Dreadnought*, which had a single mast behind its forward funnel. *Bellerophon* had an unlucky early career, being damaged in a collision with the battlecruiser *Inflexible* in 1911 and subsequently with the merchant vessel *St Clair* in 1914. She served with the Home Fleet and fought at Jutland in 1916. After World War I, she was converted to a gunnery training ship and scrapped under the terms of the Washington Treaty of the 1920s.

SPECIFICATIONS

COUNTRY OF ORIGIN United Kingdom
CREW: 735
WEIGHT: 22,245 tonnes (22,102 tons)
DIMENSIONS: 160.3m x 25.2m x 8.3m (526ft 6in x 82ft 6in x 278ft 3in)
RANGE: 10,296km (5720nm) at 12 knots
ARMOUR: 254–380mm (10–15in) belt, 203mm (8in) bulkheads
ARMAMENT: 10 x 305mm (12in), 16 x 102mm (4in) guns, three torpedo tubes
POWERPLANT: four-shaft, geared steam turbines
PERFORMANCE: 21 knots

Ben-my-Chree

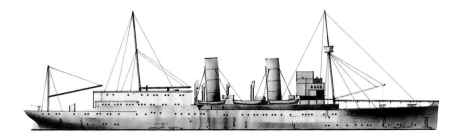

Ben-my-Chree, a former passenger vessel on the Isle of Man route, was converted into a seaplane carrier in 1915. She was fitted with a large hangar aft, plus a flying-off ramp on the fore deck. She was equipped with the new Sopwith Schneider seaplane fighters. This aircraft had a 100hp (75kW) rotary engine, an upward-firing Lewis gun and the ability to climb to 3048m (10,000ft) in a little over 30 minutes. With such improvements as these, the Sopwith Schneider presented the first serious threat to the Zeppelin airships which were attacking targets in the UK. Later, armed with two torpedo-carrying Short seaplanes, Ben-my-Chree served in the Dardanelles campaign, her aircraft sinking two Turkish vessels. While anchored in Kastelorgio harbour in 1917, Ben-my-Chree was attacked by Turkish shore batteries and sunk.

SPECIFICATIONS
COUNTRY OF ORIGIN United Kingdom
CREW: 250
WEIGHT: 3942 tonnes (3880 tons)
DIMENSIONS: 114m x 14m x 5.3m (374ft x 46ft x 17ft 6in)
RANGE: 2223km (1200nm) at 10 knots
ARMOUR: none
ARMAMENT: 4 x short 184 seaplanes
POWERPLANT: twin-screw turbines
PERFORMANCE: 24.5 knots

Benbow

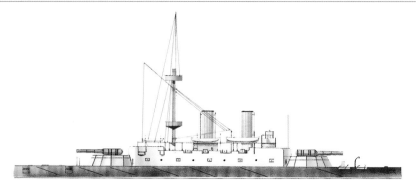

Benbow was one of the Rodney class of battleship built in answer to the French Formidable class then under construction. Original armament was to have been four 343mm (13.5in) and eight 152mm (6in) guns, but the Woolwich Arsenal was unable to deliver these and so two 112-tonne (111-ton) guns were mounted instead, in large open barbettes, one fore and one aft. The weight saved was used to install an extra pair of 152mm (6in) guns. There were many problems with the main armament, and the entire battleship class was delayed, Benbow herself taking six years to complete. Benbow was named after Admiral John Benbow (1653–1702) who was killed in action in the West Indies. The warship spent most of her active service life in the Mediterranean before being paid off in 1904. She was scrapped in 1909.

SPECIFICATIONS

COUNTRY OF ORIGIN United Kingdom
CREW: 523
WEIGHT: 10,770 tonnes (10,600 tons)
DIMENSIONS: 99m x 21m x 8.2m (325ft x 69ft x 27ft 10in)
RANGE: 9265km (5000nm) at 8 knots
ARMOUR: 450–203mm (18–8in) belt, 400–178mm (16–7in) bulkheads, 356–304mm (14–12in) barbettes
ARMAMENT: 2 x 412mm (16.25in), 10 x 152mm (6in) guns
POWERPLANT: twin-screw inverted compound engines
PERFORMANCE: 17.5 knots

Benedetto Brin

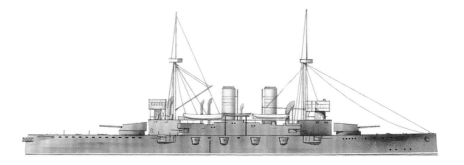

Benedetto Brin was designed by one of the world's leading naval architects at the time and, on completion, was named after him. The warship's design was a compromise, with her protection being reduced in favour of both speed and firepower. Benedetto Brin and her sister Regina Margherita were unique ships and had good sea-keeping capabilities. Launched in 1901 and completed in 1905, the warship Benedetto Brin was involved in naval operations off Tripoli in 1911 and subsequently in the Aegean Sea in the following year. On 27 September 1915, Benedetto Brin was destroyed by a magazine explosion in Brindisi harbour, either as a result of Austrian sabotage or of an accident involving unstable cordite. About half her crew (421 men) perished in the incident.

SPECIFICATIONS

COUNTRY OF ORIGIN Italy
CREW: 812–900
WEIGHT: 13,426 tonnes (13,215 tons
DIMENSIONS: 138.6m x 23.8m x 8.8m (449ft 6in x 78ft 3in x 29ft)
RANGE: 18,000km (10,000nm) at 12 knots
ARMOUR: 152mm (6in) side, 76mm (3in) deck, 203mm (8in) turrets
ARMAMENT: 4 x 304mm (12in), 4 x 203mm (8in), 12 x 152mm (6in) guns
POWERPLANT: twin-screw, triple expansion engines
PERFORMANCE: 20.3 knots

Berlin

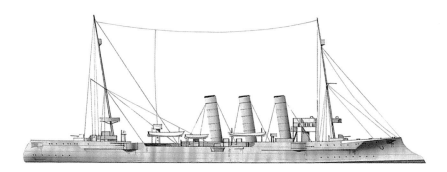

Berlin was a Brandenburg frigate of medium size developed from the larger and slower ships of the line. They were built as a consequence of the growing need for a special vessel to carry out fast scouting work, with sufficient speed to outrun the sloops that were usually deployed as lookouts for a main battle fleet. Frigates were never intended to fight the standard ships of the line, but were employed in cruising the world's oceans, protecting the commercial trade of their own country and attacking that of the enemy. Berlin was a good sea boat, and the experience gained from her performance led other countries to develop their own frigates along similar lines. These vessels grew from ships carrying around 20 cannon to larger types mounting over 40 guns on a single deck. The term 'frigate' lapsed from naval terminology in the 19th century, and did not reappear until World War II.

SPECIFICATIONS
COUNTRY OF ORIGIN Germany
CREW: 375
WEIGHT: 1016 tonnes (1000 tons)
DIMENSIONS: 48.7m x 11.5m (160ft x 38ft)
RANGE: unlimited, depending on provisions
ARMOUR:
ARMAMENT: 20 x 24-pounder guns
POWERPLANT:
PERFORMANCE: 4 knots

Bismarck

The 1919 Treaty of Versailles imposed tight restrictions on German naval developments. In spite of this, the Germans managed to carry out secret design studies and, when the Anglo-German Naval Treaty of 1935 came into force, were able to respond quickly. They began the construction of two battleships, *Bismark* and *Tirpitz*. As they had been unable to properly test new hull forms, they used the World War I *Baden* design. While they were equipped with powerful modern engines and were fine, well-armed warships, the dated armour configuration meant that the steering gear and much of the communications and control systems were poorly protected. In May 1941, *Bismark* was sent on a raiding mission into the Atlantic, but the Royal Navy caught up with her. In the ensuing battles she sunk *Hood*, before suffering so much damage that her crew scuttled her.

SPECIFICATIONS

COUNTRY OF ORIGIN Germany
CREW: 2039
WEIGHT: 50,955 tonnes (50,153 tons)
DIMENSIONS: 250m x 36m x 9m (823ft 6in x 118ft 1in x 29ft 6in)
RANGE: 15,000km (8100nm) at 18 knots
ARMOUR: 312–262mm (12.5–10.5in) belt, 362–178mm (14.5–7in) main turrets
ARMAMENT: 8 x 380mm (15in), 12 x 152mm (6in) guns, six aircraft
POWERPLANT: three-shaft geared turbines
PERFORMANCE: 29 knots

Bretagne

Because France found herself falling behind in the dreadnought naval race, *Bretagne* and her sisters *Provence* and *Lorraine* were based on the design of the preceding Courbet class to cut down construction time. *Bretagne* served in the Mediterranean from 1916–18, then underwent a series of extensive modernizations in 1921–23, 1927–30 and 1932–35. With the surrender of France in 1940, *Bretagne* and other French naval warships were called upon to join a British alliance, but the French Admiral Gensoul refused. British warships, their gunfire directed by Swordfish spotter aircraft from the carrier *Ark Royal*, opened fire on the French vessels in their anchorage at Oran in Algeria. Heavy shells tore into the magazine of *Bretagne*, which blew up and capsized with the loss of 1012 lives.

SPECIFICATIONS

COUNTRY OF ORIGIN France
CREW: 1133
WEIGHT: 29,420 tonnes (28,956 tons)
DIMENSIONS: 166m x 27m x 10m (544ft 8in x 88ft 3in x 32ft 2in)
RANGE: 8460km (4700nm) at 10 knots
ARMOUR: 279mm (11in) belt, 254–380mm (10–15in) turrets
ARMAMENT: 10 x 340mm (13.4in) guns
POWERPLANT: quadruple-screw geared turbines
PERFORMANCE: 20 knots

Canada

In 1911, Chile had two new battleships under construction, but all work on these vessels ceased in 1914 and *Almirante Latorre*, the most advanced of the two, was subsequently bought by the Royal Navy and renamed *Canada*. Her sister ship, the *Almirante Cochrane*, was also taken over by the British and renamed *Eagle*. *Canada* was a lengthened 'Iron Duke' type battleship. She had two large unequal funnels and a high tripod foremast and pole mainmast. Completed in 1915, *Canada* spent her entire war service with the Grand Fleet at Scapa Flow. She was one of the most effective battleships in the fleet; seeing action at the Battle of Jutland in 1916, and she took part in the blockade of Germany. *Canada* was returned to Chile in 1920 and continued to see service as one of that country's capital ships.

SPECIFICATIONS

COUNTRY OF ORIGIN: Chile
CREW: 1176
WEIGHT: 32,634 tonnes (32,120 tons)
DIMENSIONS: 202m x 28m x 9m (660ft 9in x 92ft x 29ft 6in)
RANGE: 8153km (4400nm) at 10 knots
ARMOUR: 229–112mm (9–4.5in) belt, 254mm (10in) barbettes, 152mm (6in) turrets
ARMAMENT: 10 x 355mm (14in) guns
POWERPLANT: quadruple-screw geared turbines
PERFORMANCE: 22.8 knots

Canberra

Originally commissioned in 1941 as a Baltimore class cruiser, *Canberra* saw much war service in the central Pacific from 1944, in the battle for Truk and in heavy raids on Japanese-held islands as part of the US Task Group 58. In October 1944, she was badly damaged by a torpedo off Okinawa. She was rebuilt and recommissioned in 1955 as one of two Boston class missile cruisers. *Canberra* and her sister, *Boston*, were the first US Navy vessels specifically designed as anti-aircraft missile ships and were rushed into service during the Cold War. Armed with Terrier missiles in place of their aft turrets, their forward turrets were also to be replaced with missiles, though this never occurred. Instead, other ships were converted to increase the US Navy's anti-aircraft missile capability. *Canberra* was stricken in 1973.

SPECIFICATIONS

COUNTRY OF ORIGIN: United States
CREW: 1544
WEIGHT: 18,234 tonnes (17,947 tons)
DIMENSIONS: 205.4m x 21.25m x 7.6m (673ft 5in x 69ft 8in x 24ft 11in)
RANGE: 13,140km (7300nm) at 12 knots
ARMOUR: 51mm (2in) belt
ARMAMENT: 2 x Terrier surface-to-air missiles (72 missiles per launcher), 6 x 203mm (8in), 10 x 127mm (5in) guns
POWERPLANT: four-shaft geared turbines
PERFORMANCE: 33 knots

Charles de Gaulle (CVN)

In September 1980, the French government approved the construction of two nuclear-powered aircraft carriers to replace its two conventionally powered 'Clemenceau'-class carriers dating back to the 1950s. However, the French CVN programme was bedevilled by political opposition and technical problems, both with the vessel and the aircraft. The first ship of the class, FS *Charles de Gaulle*, was laid down in April 1989 and launched in May 1994, but commissioned only in May 2001. The *Charles de Gaulle* is equipped with a hangar for 20–25 aircraft (around half the air group) and carries the same reactor units as the 'Le Triomphant'-class SSBN, which permits five years of continuous steaming at 25 knots before refuelling. She saw active service in Operation *Enduring Freedom* in 2001, flying missions against al-Qaeda targets. She had a 15-month refit in 2007–08 including new propellers, but required further repairs in 2009.

SPECIFICATIONS

COUNTRY OF ORIGIN: France
CREW: 1350; air wing 600
WEIGHT: 42,672 tonnes (42,000 tons)
DIMENSIONS: 261.5m x 64.36m x 9.43m (858ft x 211ft 2in x 30ft 10in)
RANGE: unlimited distance; 20 years
ARMOUR: unknown
ARMAMENT: 4 x 8 cell SYLVER launchers carrying the MBDA Aster 15 surface-to-air missile; 2 x 6 cell Sadral launchers carrying Mistral short range: missiles; 8 x Giat 20F2 20mm (0.79in) cannons; 40 x aircraft
POWERPLANT: 2 x K15 pressurized water reactors (PWR)
PERFORMANCE: 27 knots

Clémenceau

Clémenceau was one of three French battleships laid down between 1935 and 1939. The others were *Richelieu* and *Jean Bart*; a fourth, *Gascoigne*, was ordered but later cancelled. When France fell in 1940, the Germans found *Clémenceau*'s incomplete hull in dock at Brest. When the Allies invaded France, the Germans considered using it to block the harbour entrance, but she was sunk during a bombing raid in August 1944. The illustration shows her as she would have looked if completed according to the 1940 plans. Her two sister ships both saw service; *Richelieu* was taken over by the Allies and served in the Indian Ocean in 1944–45, and *Jean Bart*, having been damaged by gunfire during the Allied landings in North Africa in 1942, was completed after the war and took part in the Anglo-French Suez operations in 1956.

SPECIFICATIONS

COUNTRY OF ORIGIN: France
CREW: 1550
WEIGHT: 48,260 tonnes (47,500 tons)
DIMENSIONS: 247.9m x 33m x 9.6m (813ft 2in x 108ft 3in x 31ft 7in)
RANGE: (est) 15,750km (8500nm) at 14 knots
ARMOUR: 337–243mm (13.5–9.75in) belt
ARMAMENT: 8 x 381mm (15in) guns
POWERPLANT: quadruple-screw, geared turbines
PERFORMANCE: (est) 25 knots

Colossus

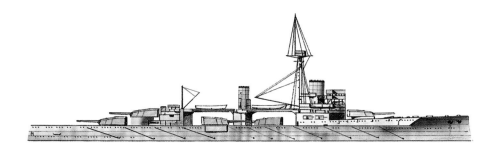

Colossus and her sister ship, *Hercules*, formed part of the rapid British naval expansion programme of 1909. *Colossus* had an improvement over previous dreadnoughts in that she was built with stronger armour protection. To save weight, the aftermast was omitted, but the foremast – with its vital fire control centre – was placed behind the first funnel, although this meant that she suffered severely from smoke interference. *Colossus* was one of the last British battleships to mount 305mm (12in) guns; the next major group would carry the new 343mm (13.5in) weapons. During the Battle of Jutland in 1916, where she was flagship of the Battle Fleet's 5th Division, she was hit by two shells. *Colossus* subsequently served as a cadet training ship before being sold for scrap and broken up at Alloa, Scotland, in 1922.

SPECIFICATIONS

COUNTRY OF ORIGIN: United Kingdom
CREW: 755
WEIGHT: 23,419 tonnes (23,050 tons)
DIMENSIONS: 166m x 26m x 9m (544ft 7in x 85ft 4in x 28ft 9in)
RANGE: 12,024km (6680nm) at 12 knots
ARMOUR: 279–178mm (11–7in) belt, 279–102mm (11–4in) barbettes
ARMAMENT: 10 x 305mm (12in) guns
POWERPLANT: four-shaft turbines
PERFORMANCE: 21 knots

Conqueror

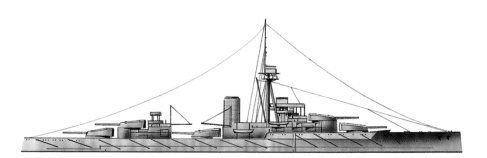

An increase in displacement over the previous class enabled *Conqueror* and her three sisters to mount the new 343mm (13.5in) guns, making these vessels the first of the so-called 'superdreadnoughts'. *Conqueror* also carried the 533mm (21in) torpedo instead of the 450mm (18in) version. While she featured a more sleek design than the early dreadnoughts, there was one major weakness in *Conqueror*'s layout. The vitally important fire control mast was positioned between the funnels, resulting in severe smoke interference at high speeds. In December 1914, she was damaged in collision with the battleship *Monarch*; after repair, she rejoined the Grand Fleet and fought in the Battle of Jutland in 1916. She was sold and broken up in 1922. Her sister ships were *Monarch*, *Orion* and *Thunderer*.

SPECIFICATIONS

COUNTRY OF ORIGIN: United Kingdom
CREW: 752
WEIGHT: 26,284 tonnes (25,870 tons)
DIMENSIONS: 177m x 27m x 9m (581ft x 88ft 7in x 29ft 6in)
RANGE: 12,470km (6730nm) at 10 knots
ARMOUR: 304–203mm (12–8in) waterline belt, 280mm (11.2in) on turrets
ARMAMENT: 10 x 343mm (13.5in) guns
POWERPLANT: quadruple-shaft turbines
PERFORMANCE: 21 knots

Conte di Cavour

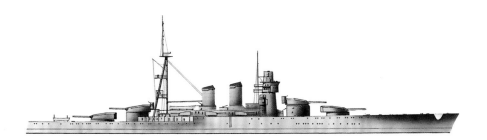

Conte di Cavour was designed in 1908 as an improved version of *Dante Alighieri*. Completed in 1914, *Conte di Cavour* saw war service in the southern Adriatic and, in 1919, she engaged in a cruise to the US. In 1923, she operated in support of Italian troops occupying the island of Corfu. She was extensively rebuilt between 1933 and 1937 and emerged as a virtually new ship. *Conte di Cavour* had new machinery and her hull was lengthened. Sunk at Taranto by torpedoes launched from British aircraft flying from *Illustrious*, *Conte di Cavour* was later refloated and towed to Trieste. She was rebuilt, but, following the Italian surrender, she was seized by the Germans in September 1943, and eventually sunk during an air raid in 1945. Her wreckage was broken up at the end of World War II.

SPECIFICATIONS

COUNTRY OF ORIGIN: Italy
CREW: 1200
WEIGHT: 29,496 tonnes (29,032 tons)
DIMENSIONS: 186m x 28m x 9m (611ft 6in x 91ft 10in x 29ft 6in)
RANGE: 8640km (4800nm) at 10 knots
ARMOUR: 254mm (10in) side and turrets
ARMAMENT: 10 x 320mm (12.6in), 12 x 120mm (4.7in) guns
POWERPLANT: twin-screw turbines
PERFORMANCE: 28.2 knots

Courageous

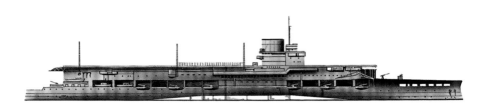

Courageous and her sister, *Glorious*, were completed in 1917 as fast cruisers for service in the Baltic. They were heavily armed with four 380mm (15in) guns, but had very little armour. By the 1920s, Britain was anxious to increase her carrier strength, so both vessels, and their near-sister *Furious*, were converted to aircraft carriers. The conversion of *Courageous* was completed in March 1928. Her superstructure and armament were replaced by an aircraft hangar running almost the length of the ship. The forward 18m (59ft) of the hangar was an open deck, which could be used to fly off slow-flying aircraft such as the Swordfish. Above this was an open flight deck, with two large elevators set into it. All three ships served through the 1930s, and formed the backbone of the British carrier force at the start of World War II. In the opening days of the war, *Courageous* was torpedoed and sunk by U20.

SPECIFICATIONS

COUNTRY OF ORIGIN: United Kingdom
CREW: 828
WEIGHT: 26,517 tonnes (26,100 tons)
DIMENSIONS: 240m x 27m x 8m (786ft 5in x 90ft 6in x 27ft 3in)
RANGE: 5929km (3200nm) at 19 knots
ARMOUR: 75–50mm (3–2in) belt
ARMAMENT: 16 x 120mm (4.7in) guns, 6 x flights of aircraft
POWERPLANT: quadruple-screw turbines
PERFORMANCE: 31.5 knots

Dante Alighieri

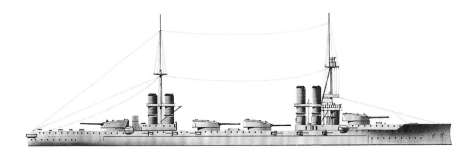

Designed by Engineering Admiral Masdea, *Dante Alighieri* was the first battleship to mount triple turrets on the centreline; she was also the first Italian dreadnought to be built. Laid down in 1909, she was completed in 1912. *Dante Alighieri* was reconstructed in 1923 and given a tripod mast. In World War I, she was the flagship of the Italian Fleet in the southern Adriatic, although she saw no action. When Italy entered the war in 1915, the fleet included six dreadnoughts, with four more under construction. The main operational base was originally Trieste, but the main body of the fleet later moved to Taranto to escape Austrian air attacks. Although the Italian battle fleet did little during the war, its ships carried out a successful blockade of the eastern Adriatic coastline. *Dante Alighieri* was scrapped in 1928.

SPECIFICATIONS

COUNTRY OF ORIGIN: Italy
CREW: 981
WEIGHT: 22,149 tonnes (21,800 tons)
DIMENSIONS: 168m x 26.5m x 10m (551ft 2in x 87ft 3in x 31ft 10in)
RANGE: 9265km (5000nm) at 10 knots
ARMOUR: 152–249mm (6–9.8in) on belt
ARMAMENT: 12 x 304mm (12in), 20 x 120mm (4.7in) guns
POWERPLANT: quadruple-screw turbines
PERFORMANCE: 22 knots

Danton

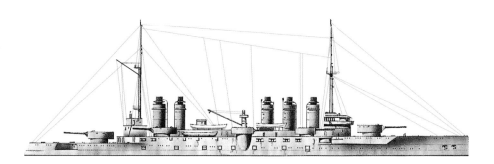

Danton and her five sisters were the last battleships to be built for the French Navy before the British all-big-gun battleship *Dreadnought* appeared on the scene and revolutionized naval development. Although *Danton*'s class contained powerful vessels, it was too late to provide a serious challenge to the dreadnoughts then entering service. Named after Georges Jacques Danton, a leader of the French Revolution, the battleship was laid down at Brest in 1908 and launched in July 1909. She was completed in 1911 and saw initial war service in escorting Mediterranean convoys. In 1915, *Danton* was on station in the Adriatic and in 1916 in the Aegean. On 19 March 1917, en route from Toulon to Corfu, she was hit by two torpedoes from the German submarine U64 and sank southwest of Sardinia with the loss of 296 lives.

SPECIFICATIONS

COUNTRY OF ORIGIN: France
CREW: 753, later 923
WEIGHT: 19,761 tonnes (19,450 tons)
DIMENSIONS: 146.5m x 25.8m x 9m (480ft 8in x 84ft 8in x 28ft 8in)
RANGE: 6066km (3370nm) at 10 knots
ARMOUR: 270mm (10.8in) belt, 300mm (11.75in) main turrets
ARMAMENT: 4 x 304mm (12in) guns
POWERPLANT: quadruple-screw turbines
PERFORMANCE: 19.3 knots

Dédalo

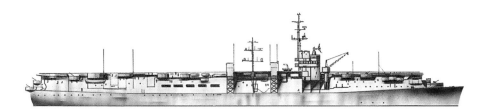

Dédalo was formerly the US Navy ship *Cabot*, which had been laid down in 1942 as a cruiser, but completed the following year as a carrier of the Independence class. After service in World War II, *Cabot* was decommissioned in 1947. In 1967 she was lent to Spain, who purchased her in 1972, renaming her *Dédalo*. Her normal air wing comprised four air groups, one with eight Matador (Harrier) V/STOL aircraft, one with four Sea King ASW helicopters, one with four Agusta-Bell 212 ASW/electronic warfare helicopters, and one with four specialised helicopters (for example, Bell AH-1G attack helicopters to support an amphibious landing.) A maximum of seven four-aircraft groups could be handled aboard the carrier. She remained in service until the carrier *Principe de Asturias* entered service in 1987.

SPECIFICATIONS
COUNTRY OF ORIGIN: Spain
CREW: 1112
WEIGHT: 16,678 tonnes (16,416 tons)
DIMENSIONS: 190m x 22m x 8m (622ft 4in x 72ft 2in x 26ft 3in)
RANGE: 13,500km (7500nm) at 12 knots
ARMOUR: 127mm (5in) belt
ARMAMENT: 26 x 40mm (1.6in) guns, 7 x VSTOL aircraft, 20 x helicopters
POWERPLANT: quadruple-screw turbines
PERFORMANCE: 30 knots

Derfflinger

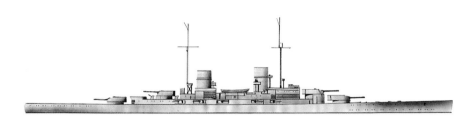

On 16 December 1914, *Derfflinger* was part of a force of German warships that bombarded Scarborough and Whitby on the northeast coast of England. Shortly afterwards, in January 1915, she was seriously damaged in the Battle of Dogger Bank. In the following year, 1916, *Derfflinger* took part in the Battle of Jutland and blew up the British battlecruiser *Queen Mary* with 11 salvos. However, during that same battle, she was hit by ten 380mm (15in) and ten 304mm (12in) shells. Despite fires on board, severe flooding and damage to her after-turrets, she survived the battle. *Derfflinger* and her two sister ships, *Hindenburg* and *Lutzow*, all of which had been launched in 1913, were arguably the best capital ships of their day. *Derfflinger* was scuttled at Scapa Flow in 1919 and raised for scrap in 1934.

SPECIFICATIONS

COUNTRY OF ORIGIN: Germany
CREW: 1112
WEIGHT: 30,706 tonnes (30,223 tons)
DIMENSIONS: 210m x 29m x 8m (689ft x 95ft 2in x 27ft 3in)
RANGE: 10,080km (5600nm) at 12 knots
ARMOUR: 300mm (11.8in) waterline belt
ARMAMENT: 8 x 304mm (12in) guns
POWERPLANT: quadruple-screw turbines
PERFORMANCE: 28 knots

Deutschland

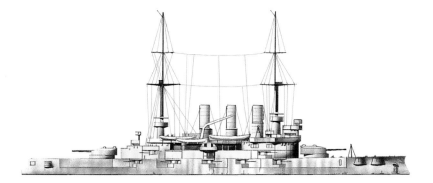

Deutschland was part of Germany's last pre-dreadnought class laid down between 1903 and 1905. They differed slightly from the previous class in that they had more 89mm (3.5in) guns plus improved protection, but other weaknesses remained as was demonstrated at the Battle of Jutland in 1916, when one vessel in the class, *Pommern*, suffered a magazine explosion after only one hit from a torpedo. Small tube boilers were used for the Deutschland class, and these became standard for all vessels employed in the German Navy. Two ships of the class, *Schlesien* and *Schleswig-Holstein*, survived to serve in World War II and were lost in action. *Schleswig-Holstein* was sunk in an air attack in December 1944, and *Schlesien* ran on a mine in the Baltic in April 1945. *Deutschland* was scrapped in 1922.

SPECIFICATIONS

COUNTRY OF ORIGIN: Germany
CREW: 743
WEIGHT: 14,216 tonnes (13,993 tons)
DIMENSIONS: 127.6m x 22m x 8m (418ft 8in x 72ft 2in x 26ft 3in)
RANGE: 8894km (4800nm) at 12 knots
ARMOUR: 248mm (9.75in) belt, 280mm (11in) on main turrets
ARMAMENT: 14 x 170mm (6.7in), 4 x 279mm (11in) guns
POWERPLANT: twin-screw, triple expansion engines
PERFORMANCE: 18.5 knots

Dixmude

Dixmude was one of three escort carriers which were built in the US for lease to Britain. The carrier's original name was *Rio Parana*. Launched in 1940, the flight deck was increased to 134 metres (440ft) on arrival in Britain and, in 1942, her US weapons were replaced with British 102mm (4in) Mk V guns. Renamed *Biter*, she mostly served on convoy escort duties. Escort carriers such as the *Biter* did much to turn the Battle of the Atlantic in the Allies' favour. She was returned to the US in 1945 and handed over to France, where she became the *Dixmude* and served as an aircraft transport. She saw action in Indo-China during 1946–48. In the early 1950s, she was disarmed, and in 1960 she was hulked as an accommodation ship. *Dixmude* was returned to the US in 1966 and subsequently scrapped.

SPECIFICATIONS
COUNTRY OF ORIGIN: France
CREW: 555
WEIGHT: 11,989 tonnes (11,800 tons)
DIMENSIONS: 150m x 23m x 7.6m (490ft 10in x 75ft 6in x 25ft 2in)
RANGE: 7412km (4000nm) at 15 knots
ARMOUR: 50–100mm (2–4in)
ARMAMENT: 3 x 102mm (4in) guns, 15 x aircraft
POWERPLANT: single-screw diesel engines
PERFORMANCE: 16.5 knots

Dreadnought

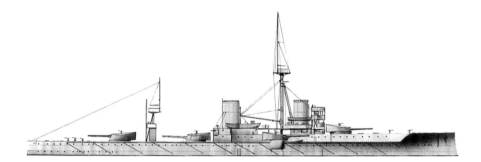

With the launch of *Dreadnought* in 1906, a new and more advanced era of warship construction began. *Dreadnought* was the first 'all-big-gun' battleship, so much so that she made all existing battleships obsolete. *Dreadnought* saw active service in World War I, being surpassed only by even larger ships of her type, to which she gave her generic name. Despite her warlike reputation, during World War I she only sank one enemy vessel, a German submarine which she rammed. The Royal Navy's Dreadnought fleet at the outbreak of World War I was thinly stretched, and after two months of hostilities, ships had to be sent to their home ports on the south coast for refit. This meant that two or three of the Grand Fleet's most important vessels were absent from active duty at any one time. *Dreadnought* was scrapped in 1923.

SPECIFICATIONS
COUNTRY OF ORIGIN: United Kingdom
CREW: 695-773
WEIGHT: 22,194 tonnes (21,845 tons)
DIMENSIONS: 160.4m x 25m x 8m (526ft 3in x 82ft x 26ft 3in)
RANGE: 11,916km (6620nm) at 10 knots
ARMOUR: 203–279mm (8–11in) belt, 280mm (11in) on turrets
ARMAMENT: 10 x 304mm (12in) guns
POWERPLANT: quadruple-screw turbines
PERFORMANCE: 21.6 knots

Duilio

Completed in 1916 as members of the Doria class, *Duilio* and her sister *Andrea Doria* underwent several changes in their careers, for example, receiving seaplanes in 1925. Extensive modernization between 1937 and 1940 upgraded both their armour and guns and turned both vessels into virtually new ships. *Duilio* was damaged in the British air attack on Taranto naval base, in November 1940. She was towed to Genoa for repair and narrowly escaped further damage when the port was bombarded by British warships in February 1941. Returned to active service later that year, she was employed on convoy interception and escort duty before being placed on the Reserve in 1942. After her surrender to the Allies at Malta in September 1943, *Duilio* was used as a training ship. She was broken up at La Spezia in 1957.

SPECIFICATIONS

COUNTRY OF ORIGIN: Italy
CREW: 1198
WEIGHT: 29,861 tonnes (29,391 tons)
DIMENSIONS: 187m x 28m x 8.5m (613ft 2in x 91ft 10in x 28ft 2in)
RANGE: 8640km (4800nm) at 12 knots
ARMOUR: 254mm (10in) on sides, 279mm (11in) on turrets
ARMAMENT: 10 x 320mm (12.6in) guns
POWERPLANT: twin-screw turbines
PERFORMANCE: 27 knots

Dunkerque

Based on the British Nelson class battleships, *Dunkerque* was the first French warship to be laid down after the Washington Treaty of 1922. She was the culmination of a series of design studies that resulted in an answer to the German Deutschland class of the early 1930s. A hangar and a catapult were provided for the four scout planes which she was to carry. In October 1939, as flagship of the Brest-based Force L, she joined the Royal Navy in the hunt for the German pocket battleship *Admiral Graf Spee*. She was employed on convoy escort duty until the surrender of France and, in July 1940, she was severely damaged by British warships at Mers-el-Kébir and by a torpedo attack three days later, with the loss of 210 lives. *Dunkerque* was scuttled in Toulon harbour in 1942, and raised and sold for scrap in 1953.

SPECIFICATIONS
COUNTRY OF ORIGIN: France
CREW: 1431
WEIGHT: 36,068 tonnes (35,500 tons)
DIMENSIONS: 214.5m x 31m x 8.6m (703ft 9in x 102ft 3in x 28ft 6in)
RANGE: 13,897km (7500nm) at 15 knots
ARMOUR: 243–143mm (9.75–5.75in) main belt, 331–152mm (13.25–6in) on turrets
ARMAMENT: 16 x 127mm (5in), 8 x 330mm (13in) guns
POWERPLANT: quadruple-screw turbines
PERFORMANCE: 29.5 knots

Eagle (1924)

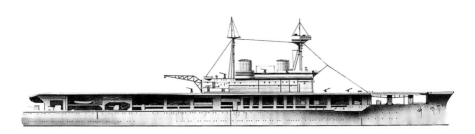

Eagle was originally laid down in 1913 as the Chilean Navy's super-dreadnought *Almirante Cochrane*. Work stopped with the outbreak of World War I, and it only began again in 1917 after her purchase by the Royal Navy. Construction of the ship then continued, and the vessel was turned into an aircraft carrier. Eventually, she entered service in 1924. When Italy entered the war on the Axis side in June 1940, *Eagle* was the only aircraft carrier at the disposal of the British in the Mediterranean, and she performed sterling service in ferrying fighter aircraft to the besieged island of Malta. She had previously operated in the Indian Ocean and the South Atlantic, based in Ceylon, her main task being to search for German commerce raiders. In August 1942, *Eagle* was sunk in the Mediterranean by U73 while attempting to deliver aircraft to Malta.

SPECIFICATIONS

COUNTRY OF ORIGIN: United Kingdom
CREW: 950
WEIGHT: 27,664 tonnes (27,229 tons)
DIMENSIONS: 203.4m x 32m x 8m (667ft 6in x 105ft x 26ft 3in)
RANGE: 5559km (3000nm) at 15 knots
ARMOUR: 112–25mm (4.5–1in) belt, 100mm (4in) bulkhead, 37.5–25mm (1.5–1in) decks
ARMAMENT: 5 x 102mm (4in), 9 x 152mm (6in) guns, 21 x aircraft
POWERPLANT: quadruple-screw turbines
PERFORMANCE: 22.5 knots

Eagle (1951)

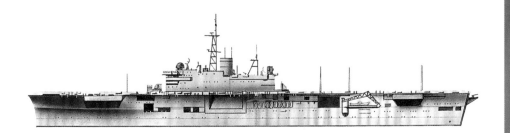

With the completion of the naval construction programmes of 1936 and 1937 and with the construction of the Illustrious class carriers of 1938 in progress, designs were prepared in 1942 for their successors. These designs allowed for two complete hangars to be built together with the ability to handle the heavier aircraft that were expected to be introduced. *Eagle* entered service in October 1951, was decommissioned in January 1972, and was sent for breaking-up in 1978. She was the sister ship of HMS *Ark Royal*. During her service career she took part in many peacekeeping actions, but she is perhaps best remembered for her offensive role in the Anglo-French Suez operations, when her aircraft carried out numerous strikes on targets in the Suez Canal Zone in support of Anglo-French ground forces.

SPECIFICATIONS

COUNTRY OF ORIGIN: United Kingdom
CREW: 2740
WEIGHT: 47,200 tonnes (46,452 tons)
DIMENSIONS: 245m x 34m x 11m (803ft 9in x 112ft 9in x 36ft 1in)
RANGE: 7412km (4000nm) at 20 knots
ARMOUR: 112mm (4.5in) belt, 112–37.5mm (4.5–1.5in) bulkheads
ARMAMENT: 16 x 112mm (4.5in) guns
POWERPLANT: quadruple-screw turbines
PERFORMANCE: 32 knots

Emanuele Filiberto

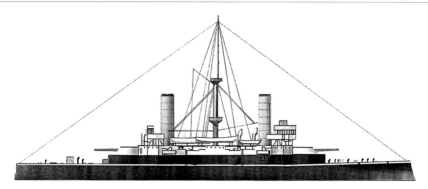

Emanuele Filiberto was laid down in 1893, launched in 1897, and completed in 1902. However, her firepower was too light for a battleship of the line. Her speed and sea-keeping qualities were also inadequate, due to the low 4.4m (14ft 6in) freeboard forward and 3m (10ft) clearance aft. She had a high superstructure amidships, holding the twin funnels, a single military mast and her boats. Her four 254mm (10in) main guns were mounted in two armoured turrets, placed above barbettes to give clearance in heavy seas. Her secondary armament of eight 152mm (6in) guns were mounted in broadside on the main superstructure. In 1911, in the war with Turkey, she operated off Tripoli in support of Italian forces, and in 1912 formed part of the task force that occupied Rhodes. She served throughout World War I in the Adriatic. Despite her weaknesses she was not discarded until 1920.

SPECIFICATIONS

COUNTRY OF ORIGIN: Italy
CREW: 565
WEIGHT: 10,058 tonnes (9897 tons)
DIMENSIONS: 111.8m x 21m x 7.2m (366ft 10in x 69ft 3in x 23ft 10in)
RANGE: 9900km (5500nm) at 12 knots
ARMOUR: 248–122mm (9.8–4in) belt
ARMAMENT: 8 x 152mm (6in), 4 x 254mm (10in) guns, 8 x 152mm (6in)
POWERPLANT: twin-screw, triple expansion engines
PERFORMANCE: 18 knots

Engadine (1914)

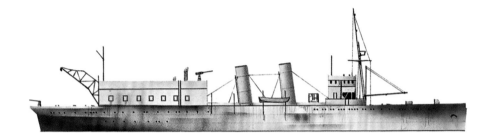

At the outbreak of World War I, the British Admiralty took over a number of fast cross-channel steamers for conversion into seaplane carriers. *Engadine* and her sister, *Riviera*, were two such ships and both were quickly converted to carry three aircraft. By December 1914, they were in action against the German airship sheds at Cuxhaven. *Engadine* was modified in 1915. She then served with the Grand Fleet, carrying out North Sea sweeps and anti-submarine patrols, and pursuing the German airships, then beginning to increase their attacks upon the British mainland. During the Battle of Jutland in 1916, a Short 184 seaplane from *Engadine* made the first-ever air reconnaissance of a fleet in action, transmitting the position of the German warships by means of wireless telegraphy. *Engadine* later served in the Mediterranean. She was returned to her owners in 1919.

SPECIFICATIONS

COUNTRY OF ORIGIN: United Kingdom
CREW: 250
WEIGHT: 1702 tonnes (1676 tons)
DIMENSIONS: 96.3m x 12.5m (316 ft x 41ft)
RANGE: 2779km (1500nm) at 18 knots
ARMOUR: 50mm (2in) belt
ARMAMENT: 2 x 102mm (4in), 1 x 6-pounder gun, 6 x seaplanes
POWERPLANT: triple-screw turbines
PERFORMANCE: 21 knots

Engadine (1967)

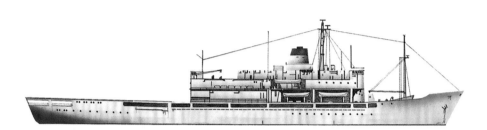

Engadine was laid down in August 1965 and was designed for the training of helicopter crews in deep-water operations. Although she does not carry her own aircraft, these can be embarked as necessary and housed in the large hangar aft of the funnel. At any one time, Engadine can carry four Wessex and two WASP helicopters, or two of the larger Sea Kings. Complement is 81, plus an additional 113 training crew. Engadine can also operate pilotless target aircraft. She is a unique vessel, giving a thorough training to the helicopter crews that form a major part of the anti-submarine defence of surface ships. Engadine forms part of the Royal Fleet Auxiliary (RFA), which consists of support vessels such as logistics ships, oilers and tankers. She is fitted with Denny Brown stabilisers to provide greater ship control during helicopter operations.

SPECIFICATIONS

COUNTRY OF ORIGIN: United Kingdom
CREW: 75 plus 113 training crews
WEIGHT: 9144 tonnes (9000 tons)
DIMENSIONS: 129.3m x 17.8m x 6.7m (424ft 3in x 58ft 5in x 22ft)
RANGE: 9265km (5000nm) at 14 knots
ARMOUR: none
ARMAMENT: ASW helicopters
POWERPLANT: single-screw diesel engines
PERFORMANCE: 16 knots

Enterprise (1938)

Early *Enterprise* designs had a flush deck, but this was thought to pose a smoke threat to landing aircraft, and an island structure to carry funnel uptakes and provide control centres was devised. The aircraft hangars were light structures independent from the hull, which could be closed off with rolling shutters. *Enterprise* was refitted in 1942 after action at the Battle of Midway, during which her dive bombers helped sink three Japanese carriers. Apart from Midway, her World War II battle honours included Guadalcanal, the Eastern Solomons, the Gilbert Islands, Kwajalein, Eniwetok, the Truk raid, Hollandia, Saipan, the Battle of the Philippine Sea, Palau, Leyte, Luzon, Taiwan, the China coast, Iwo Jima and Okinawa. She received five bomb hits and survived two attacks by kamikazes off Okinawa. She was sold in 1958, despite efforts to preserve her as a memorial.

SPECIFICATIONS
COUNTRY OF ORIGIN: United States
CREW: 2175
WEIGHT: 25,908 tonnes (25,500 tons)
DIMENSIONS: 246.7m x 26.2m x 7.9m (809ft 6in x 86ft x 26ft)
RANGE: 21,600km (12,000nm) at 12 knots
ARMOUR: 102–62.5mm (4–2.5in) belt, 37.5mm (1.5in) armoured deck 102mm (4in) bulkheads
ARMAMENT: 8 x 127mm (5in) guns
POWERPLANT: quadruple-screw turbines
PERFORMANCE: 37.5 knots

E

BATTLESHIPS AND AIRCRAFT CARRIERS 1900–PRESENT

Enterprise (1961)

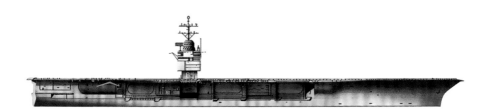

Nuclear-powered aircraft carriers had been suggested as far back as 1946, but cost delayed development of the project. *Enterprise* had a range of 643,720km (347,581nm) at 20 knots. When completed in 1961, she was the largest vessel in the world, and was the second nuclear-powered warship to enter service. Her stowage capacity was huge, including 12,240,000 litres (2,720,000 gal) of aviation fuel and 2560 tonnes (2520 tons) of aviation ordnance. She was refitted between 1979 and 1982 and given a revised island structure. *Enterprise* carries offensive tactical nuclear ordnance that includes 10kT B61, 20kT B57, 100kT B61, 330kT B61 and 900kT air-delivered gravity bombs, 10kT depth bombs; 1.4mT B43 and 1.1mT strategic nuclear weapons can also be carried as required. Her air group is similar in size and configuration to that of the Nimitz-class carriers.

SPECIFICATIONS

COUNTRY OF ORIGIN: United States
CREW: 3325 crew, 1891 air group and 71 marines
WEIGHT: 91,033 tonnes (89,600 tons)
DIMENSIONS: 335.2m x 76.8m x 10.9m (1100ft x 252ft x 36ft)
RANGE: 643,720km (400,000nm) at 20 knots
ARMOUR: classified
ARMAMENT: surface-to-air missiles, 90 aircraft
POWERPLANT: quadruple-screw geared turbines, steam supplied by 8 x nuclear reactors
PERFORMANCE: 32 knots

Erzherzog Karl

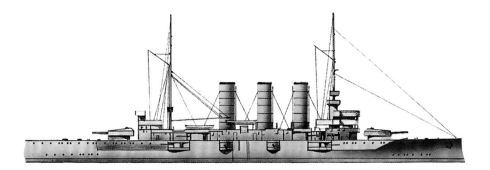

Erzherzog Karl was one of three units that formed the last of the pre-dreadnought type built for the Austrian Navy. She served in the Adriatic in World War I, and was taken over by Yugoslavia in 1919. In 1920, she was handed over to France as part of Austria's war reparations and scrapped. She is known for being the first warship to have her secondary guns housed in electrically powered turrets. The Erzherzog Karl and her sister ships, Erzherzog Ferdinand Max and Erzherzog Friedrich, were good vessels for their size, but obsolescent by the time they were completed in 1906–10. The Erzherzog Karl was named after Archduke Charles, Duke of Teschen (1771–1847), field marshal and commander of the Austrian forces against Napoleon. The Friedrich was ceded to Britain, the Ferdinand Max to France.

SPECIFICATIONS

COUNTRY OF ORIGIN: Austria
CREW: 700
WEIGHT: 10,640 tonnes (10,472 tons)
DIMENSIONS: 126.2m x 21.7m x 7.5m (414ft 2in x 71ft 6in x 24ft 8in)
RANGE: 7412km (4000nm) at 10 knots
ARMOUR: 210mm (8.4in) belt, 240mm (9.6in) turrets
ARMAMENT: 12 x 190mm (7.5in), 4 x 240mm (9.45in) guns
POWERPLANT: twin-screw, triple expansion engines
PERFORMANCE: 20.5 knots

España

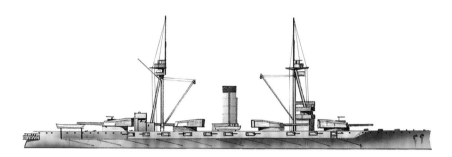

España and her two sisters combined dreadnought armament with pre-dreadnought dimensions. In 1923, *España* ran aground in fog off the Moroccan coast and could not be salvaged. *Alfonso XIII*, one of *España*'s sisters, took her name in 1931, but was sunk in 1937 when she hit a mine during the Spanish Civil War. Ironically, the mine had been laid by the Nationalists, her own side. The *España* class of small battleships were built in Spain with British technical assistance. They had four twin turrets, a single funnel and two tripod masts. The completion of one of them, *Jaime I*, was held up by World War I and she was not completed until 1921. This vessel saw more action than the others in the Spanish Civil War; she was sunk by an explosion at Cartagena in June 1937, with over 300 dead.

SPECIFICATIONS

COUNTRY OF ORIGIN: Spain
CREW: 845
WEIGHT: 15,991 tonnes (15,740 tons)
DIMENSIONS: 140m x 24m x 7.8m (459ft 4in x 78ft 9in x 25ft 7in)
RANGE: 9000km (5000nm) at 10 knots
ARMOUR: 203–75mm (8–3in) belt, plus 75mm (3in) battery, 203mm (8in) on turrets
ARMAMENT: 20 x 102mm (4in), 8 x 305mm (12in) guns
POWERPLANT: quadruple-screw turbines
PERFORMANCE: 19.5 knots

Essex

By the end of the 1930s, the increased needs of the navy for air cover led to an explosion in the size of aircraft carriers, and a larger hull was introduced to stow the aviation fuel required for the 91 aircraft now carried. There were 24 vessels in the Essex class, their designs based around an enlargement of the earlier Yorktown class carriers. *Essex* was laid down in April 1941 and entered service in 1942. She was removed from the effective list in 1969 and scrapped in 1973. *Essex*'s battle honours in World War II included raids on Marcus and Wake Islands, the Gilbert Islands and Kwajalein (1943); raids on Truk and the Marianas, Saipan, Guam, Tinian, Palau and the Battle of the Philippine Sea (1944); raids on Luzon, the China coast, the Ryukus, Iwo Jima, Okinawa and Japan (1945). In November 1944, *Essex* was damaged by a kamikaze hit at Leyte, and again in April 1945 off Okinawa.

SPECIFICATIONS

COUNTRY OF ORIGIN: United States
CREW: 2687
WEIGHT: 35,438 tonnes (34,880 tons)
DIMENSIONS: 265.7m x 29.2m x 8.3m (871ft 9in x 95ft 10in x 27ft 6in)
RANGE: 27,000km (15,000nm) at 12 knots
ARMOUR: 102–62.5mm (4–2.5in) belt and hangar deck
ARMAMENT: 12 x 127mm (5in) guns, 91 x aircraft
POWERPLANT: quadruple-screw turbines
PERFORMANCE: 32.7 knots

Flandre

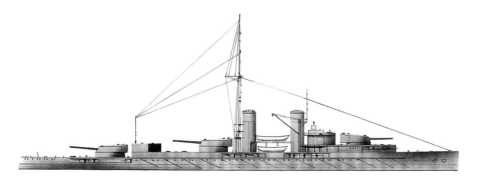

Flandre was laid down in October 1913 as one of a class of five units built in response to the increased gun calibres being used by other countries. It was decided to fit the 340mm (13.4in) guns in three quadruple turrets, which were in reality two twin mounts placed side by side in a single well-armoured barbette. Work halted on the class in 1914 and they were launched to clear the docks. Four were scrapped in 1924–25; one of the class, Béarn, was completed as an aircraft carrier. Impounded by the Americans at Martinique after going aground, Flandre was towed to Puerto Rico. In 1943–44, she was refitted at New Orleans, rearmed, had her flight deck shortened, and was reclassified as an aircraft transport. Handed over to the Free French Navy, she saw service in the Far East in 1945–46, supporting the French reoccupation of Indo-China.

SPECIFICATIONS

COUNTRY OF ORIGIN: France
CREW: 1200
WEIGHT: 25,230 tonnes (24,833 tons)
DIMENSIONS: 176.4m x 27m x 8.7m (578ft 9in x 88ft 7in x 28ft 6in)
RANGE: 11,700km (6500nm) at 12 knots
ARMOUR: 300mm (11.8in) belt, 340–250mm (13.26–9.75in) turrets
ARMAMENT: 12 x 340mm (13.4in), 24 x 140mm (5.5in) guns
POWERPLANT: quadruple-screws; two for turbines and two for vertical triple expansion engines
PERFORMANCE: 21 knots

Florida

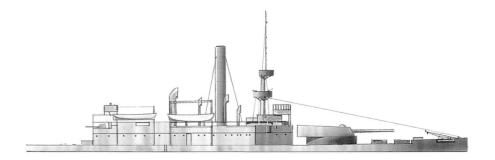

Launched in 1901, *Florida* was one of the Arkansas class of four that were the last of the big-gun monitors built for the US Navy. The maximum thickness of the belt armour was at the 37.5mm (1.5in) armoured-deck level only, tapering to 127mm (5in) at the lower edge and at the ends. The 305mm (12in) guns were in a single turret forward. Four 102mm (4in) guns were also carried, two at the rear of the superstructure and two under the bridge. All vessels of the class at some time served as submarine tenders. In 1908, she was renamed *Tallahassee* and was successively employed as an experimental ordnance ship and submarine tender. During World War I, she served in the Panama Canal Zone, the Virgin Islands and Bermuda, and from 1920 to 1922 she was used as a Reserve training ship. *Tallahassee* was sold and broken up in 1922, but her sister, *Wyoming*, was not sold until 1939.

SPECIFICATIONS

COUNTRY OF ORIGIN: United States
CREW: 270
WEIGHT: 3277 tonnes (3225 tons)
DIMENSIONS: 77.75m x 15.25m x 3.8m (255ft 1in x 50ft x 12ft 6in)
RANGE: 3113km (1680nm) at 10 knots
ARMOUR: 279–127mm (11–5in) belt, 279–229mm (11–9in) barbettes and turrets
ARMAMENT: 2 x 306mm (12in) and 4 x 102mm (4in) guns
POWERPLANT: twin screw, vertical triple expansion engines
PERFORMANCE: 12.5 knots

Foch

Laid down in 1957 and completed in 1963, *Foch* is the second of the Clémenceau class carriers. She underwent a refit between 1981 and 1982 that enabled her to carry tactical nuclear weapons, and in 1984 received a satellite communications system. Further improvements included the introduction of a point-defence missile system in place of 100mm (3.9in) guns, a new catapult mechanism and a laser landing system for her flight deck. Her missile system was improved again in 1996. Despite these upgrades, *Foch* failed to retain a full air group. From 1975, she shared one with her sister *Clémenceau* and spent part of her time as a helicopter carrier. Her strike component consisted of the Super Etendard attack aircraft, which could be armed with AN52 15kT tactical nuclear bombs. She remained in service until 2003.

SPECIFICATIONS

COUNTRY OF ORIGIN: France
CREW: 1338 (as aircraft carrier), 984 (as helicopter carrier)
WEIGHT: 32,255 tonnes (32,780 tons)
DIMENSIONS: 265m x 31.7m x 8.6m (869ft 5in x 104ft x 28ft 3in)
RANGE: 13,500km (7500nm) at 12 knots
ARMOUR: classified
ARMAMENT: 8 x 100mm (3.9in) guns, Crotale and Sadral surface-to-air missile systems, 40 x aircraft
POWERPLANT: two shaft, geared steam turbines
PERFORMANCE: 32 knots

Formidable

The 1936 Royal Navy programme called for the construction of two 23,368-tonne (23,000-ton) carriers, and at first plans were drawn up based on *Ark Royal*. With the realization that war in Europe was coming ever closer, and that such carriers would be subject to constant air attack, armour protection and defensive armament was seen as important. The aircraft hangar was set in an armoured box intended to be proof against 227kg (500lb) bombs and 152mm (6in) gunfire. *Formidable* was completed in Belfast in 1940. She received serious damage from air attack while transporting aircraft to Malta in 1941. After being repaired, she went on to serve in the Pacific and survived several kamikaze attacks. British fleet carriers had armoured flight decks, unlike their US counterparts, and were consequently far less vulnerable to air attack. She was scrapped in 1953.

SPECIFICATIONS

COUNTRY OF ORIGIN: United States
CREW: 1997
WEIGHT: 28,661 tonnes (28,210 tons)
DIMENSIONS: 226.7m x 29.1m x 8.5m (743ft 9in x 95ft 9in x 28ft)
RANGE: 20,383km (11,000nm) at 14 knots
ARMOUR: 112mm (4.5in) belt, hangars and bulkheads
ARMAMENT: 16 x 112mm (4.5in) guns, 36 x aircraft
POWERPLANT: triple-screw turbines
PERFORMANCE: 30.5 knots

Forrestal

Forrestal and her three sisters of the Forrestal class were authorized in 1951. Large size was needed to operate fast combat jets, which needed more fuel than their piston-engined predecessors. Designed with an angled flight deck and four steam catapults, *Forrestal* had space for around 3.4 million litres (750,000 gal) of aviation fuel and 1670 tonnes (1650 tons) of aviation ordnance. She served with the Atlantic Fleet until 1965, when she underwent a refit before being transferred to the Pacific Fleet for operations off Vietnam. In July 1967. she was severely damaged by fire and explosion when fire broke out on the flight deck as aircraft were being readied for operations, touching off bombs and ammunition and killing 132 crew. *Forrestal* underwent a major refit between 1983–85. She was scheduled for frontline service until the turn of the century.

SPECIFICATIONS

COUNTRY OF ORIGIN: United States
CREW: 2764 crew, 1912 air crew
WEIGHT: 80,516 tonnes (79,248 tons)
DIMENSIONS: 309.4m x 73.2m x 11.3m (1015ft 1in x 240ft 2in x 37ft 1in)
RANGE: 21,600km (12,000nm) at 10 knots
ARMOUR: classified
ARMAMENT: 8 x 127mm (5in) guns, 90 x aircraft
POWERPLANT: quadruple-screw turbines
PERFORMANCE: 33 knots

Fuji

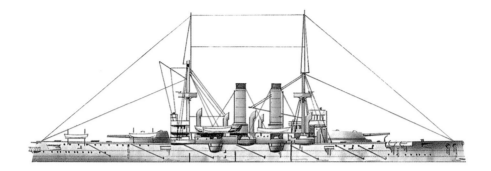

In the early 1890s, Japan anticipated war with China, and placed an order with Britain for two modern battleships. *Fuji*, and her sister, *Yashima*, were improved versions of the Royal Sovereign class, although they carried lighter but equally effective 304mm (12in) guns instead of the 344mm (13.5in) weapons of the British ships. Their main armament was placed fore and aft of the vessel, while four of the 152mm (6in) guns were mounted in casements on the main deck. These were the first modern battleships in the Japanese Navy. They were completed too late for the 1894–95 Sino-Japanese war, but took part in the 1904–05 Russo-Japanese conflict. *Yashima* was sunk by a Russian mine in May 1904, but *Fuji* survived the war. She fought in the Battle of the Yellow Sea in August 1904 and sunk the Russian battleship *Borodino* at the Battle of Tsushima in 1905. She was stricken in 1923.

SPECIFICATIONS

COUNTRY OF ORIGIN: Japan
CREW: 637
WEIGHT: 12,737 tonnes (12,533 tons)
DIMENSIONS: 125.3m x 22.3m x 8.1m (411ft 1in x 73ft 2in x 26ft 7in)
RANGE: 7412km (4000nm) at 10 knots
ARMOUR: 457–356mm (18–14in) main belt, 102mm (4in) upper belt, 356–229mm (14–9in) on barbettes
ARMAMENT: 4 x 254mm (10in), 8 x 152mm (6in) guns
POWERPLANT: twin-screw, vertical triple expanion engines
PERFORMANCE: 18 knots

Furious

The origin of one of the best-known British aircraft carriers of World War II dates back to pre-1914 when Jack Fisher – then First Sea Lord – planned for a fleet of fast, powerful cruisers with shallow draught to operate in the Baltic. *Furious* was one of three such vessels built. Launched in 1916, she was converted to a carrier in 1917 to increase the Grand Fleet's aircraft support. Originally her flight deck and hangar were built over her forward gun positions. After undergoing a more complete rebuild, *Furious* served with the Home and Mediterranean fleets in World War II. Together with HMS *Eagle*, she was an invaluable asset in the early months of the Mediterranean war, flying off fighter aircraft to Malta. Her aircraft attacked *Tirpitz* in 1944 and she was taken out of operational service the same year. She was scrapped in 1948.

SPECIFICATIONS

COUNTRY OF ORIGIN: United Kingdom
CREW: 1218
WEIGHT: 22,758 tonnes (22,400 tons)
DIMENSIONS: 239.6m x 27.4m x 7.3m (786ft 4in x 90ft x 24ft)
RANGE: 5929km (3200nm) at 19 knots
ARMOUR: 75mm (3in) belt
ARMAMENT: 6 x 102mm (4in) guns, 36 x aircraft
POWERPLANT: quadruple-screw turbines
PERFORMANCE: 30 knots

Fuso

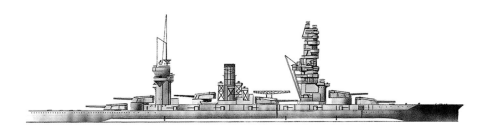

With the laying down of this vessel in March 1912 in a home yard, Japan confirmed her position as a leading naval power in the Pacific. Up until then, all Japanese battleships had been built in British yards. Although *Fuso* and her sister, *Yamarisho*, were less heavily armoured than contemporary US battleships, they carried a heavier armament and were two knots faster. As originally completed in 1915, *Fuso* had two funnels, with the first between the bridge and third turret. In an extensive refit in the 1930s, this was removed and replaced by a massive bridge structure. Underwater protection was greatly improved and new machinery fitted. *Fuso* served in the Aleutians and at Leyte during World War II, and it was during the Battle of Leyte Gulf in October 1944, that she and *Yamashiro* were sunk by gunfire and torpedoes from US battleships.

SPECIFICATIONS

COUNTRY OF ORIGIN: Japan
CREW: 1193
WEIGHT: 36,474 tonnes (35,900 tons)
DIMENSIONS: 205m x 28.7m x 8.6m (672ft 6in x 94ft 2in x 28ft 3in)
RANGE: 14,400km (8000nm)
ARMOUR: 305–102mm (12–4in) belt, 305–120mm (12–4.7in) on turrets, 203mm (8in) on barbettes
ARMAMENT: 12 x 356mm (14in), 16 x 152mm (6in) guns
POWERPLANT: quadruple-screw turbines
PERFORMANCE: 23 knots

Gambier Bay

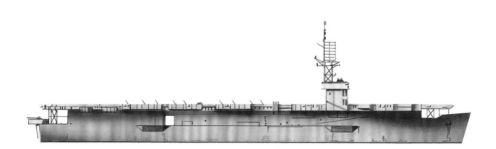

Gambier Bay was one of a 50-strong group of light escort carriers, completed from the unfinished hulls of a standard type of merchant ship mass-produced by Henry J. Kaiser in 1942. All 50 vessels were completed in under one year. The class was designed to carry an air group of nine fighters, nine bombers and nine torpedo bombers. The first mission for Gambier Bay was in early 1944, when she ferried aircraft to USS Enterprise and then supported US forces off Saipan in the Marianas and later at Leyte. She was sunk by gunfire during action off Samar in October 1944. Her loss occurred during one of the most epic sea-fights of the war, when the lightly armed escort carrier groups supporting the invasion of the Philippines fought off the main Japanese battle fleet in a surface action. The survivors of the class were all laid up at the end of the war.

SPECIFICATIONS

COUNTRY OF ORIGIN: United States
CREW: 860
WEIGHT: 11,074 tonnes (10,900 ton)
DIMENSIONS: 156.1m x 32.9m x 6.3m (512ft 3in x 108ft x 20ft 9in)
RANGE: 18,360km (10,200nm) at 12 knots
ARMOUR: 50mm (2in) belt
ARMAMENT: 1 x 127mm (5in), 16 x 40mm (1.6in) guns, 27 x aircraft
POWERPLANT: twin-screw, reciprocating engines
PERFORMANCE: 19 knots

Gangut

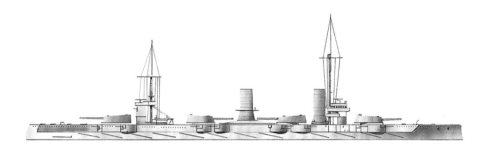

Launched in 1911, *Gangut* and her three sisters were Russia's first dreadnoughts. The contract was won by Blohm and Voss, Hamburg, but the Russian government refused funds unless they were built in Russia. As Russian industry could not produce enough high tensile steel, an ingenious construction method was used, based upon the Italian *Dante Alighieri*. Building time was lengthy, and *Gangut* was not ready until 1914, by which time she was largely obsolete. Her main guns, however, were the largest then at sea. She was renamed *Oktyabrskaya Revolutsia* in 1919. In the 'Winter War' against Finland (1939–40) she was used to bombard Finnish shore positions. In September 1941, while taking part in the defence of Leningrad, she was severely damaged by six bombs during a Stuka attack, and was again hit by four bombs in April 1942. She was scrapped in 1956–59.

SPECIFICATIONS

COUNTRY OF ORIGIN: Russia
CREW: 1126
WEIGHT: 26,264 tonnes (25,850 tons)
DIMENSIONS: 182.9m x 26.9m x 8.3m (600ft 1in x 88ft 3in x 27ft 3in)
RANGE: 7412km (4000nm) at 16 knots
ARMOUR: 226–102mm (8.9–4in) belt , 203–127mm (8–5in) on turrets, and 203mm (8in) on barbettes
ARMAMENT: 12 x 305mm (12in), 16 x 120mm (4.7in) guns
POWERPLANT: quadruple-screw turbines
PERFORMANCE: 23 knots

George Washington

George Washington is one of eight Nimitz class supercarriers built to date. She was laid down in August 1986, 17 years after Nimitz, the first of the class. George Washington carries extensive damage-control systems, including 63mm (2.5in) thick armour over parts of the hull, plus box protection over the magazines and machinery spaces. Aviation equipment includes four lifts and four steam catapults, and over 2540 tonnes (2500 tons) of aviation ordnance. The life of the nuclear reactors is 15 years. George Washington's air wing, like that of all Nimitz class carriers, comprises 90–95 aircraft, with two squadrons of Grumman F-14 Tomcats forming the interceptor element. The big carriers form the nucleus of a US fleet's Battle Force, the principal task force. Nimitz-class carriers and their associated warships have supported United Nations peacekeeping operations around the world.

SPECIFICATIONS

COUNTRY OF ORIGIN United States
CREW: 5621 crew and air group
WEIGHT: 92,950 tonnes (91,487 tons)
DIMENSIONS: 332.9m x 40.8m x 11.3m (1,092ft 2in x 133ft 10in x 37ft 1in)
RANGE: unlimited
ARMOUR: 63mm (2.5in) on hull and magazines
ARMAMENT: 4 x Vulcan 20mm (0.79in) guns plus three Sparrow surface-to-air missile launchers
POWERPLANT: quadruple-screw turbines, two water-cooled nuclear reactors
PERFORMANCE: 30 knots plus

Georgia

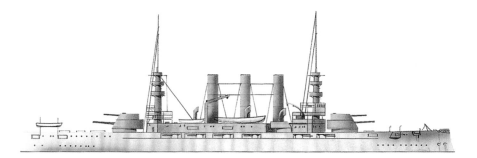

Georgia and her four sisters of the Virginia class were a major development in US battleship design. They were well-protected and carried the heaviest possible armament on a relatively modest displacement. To reduce the risk of fire damage, wood was eliminated wherever possible. Launched in 1904, *Georgia* was given cage masts in 1909–10, and was later reboilered. In 1906–07 she served with the Atlantic Fleet, and in 1907 she was damaged by a powder explosion in one of her 203mm (8in) turrets while in Cape Cod Bay. *Georgia* supported US action in Mexico in 1914 and worked with the Atlantic Fleet throughout World War I; in 1919 she made five voyages as a troop transport, bringing US personnel home from Europe, and was then transferred to the Pacific Fleet, in which she served from 1919 to 1920. She was sold in 1923.

SPECIFICATIONS

COUNTRY OF ORIGIN: United States
CREW: 812
WEIGHT: 16,351 tonnes (16,094 tons)
DIMENSIONS: 134.5m x 23.2m x 7.2m (441ft 3in x 76ft 2in x 23ft 9in)
RANGE: 9117km (4920nm) at 10 knots
ARMOUR: 279–152mm (11–6in) belt, 305–152mm (12–6in) on barbettes and turrets
ARMAMENT: 12 x 152mm (6in), 8 x 203mm (8in), 4 x 305mm (12in) guns turrets
POWERPLANT: twin-screw, vertical triple expansion engines
PERFORMANCE: 19.2 knots

Giulio Cesare

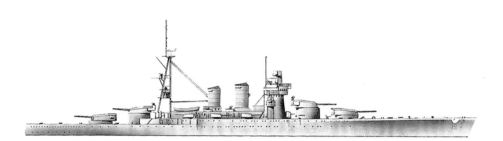

Designed in 1908 by Engineer-General Masdea, *Giulio Cesare* and her two sisters were the first large group of Italian dreadnoughts. *Giulio Cesare* was completely rebuilt between 1933 and 1937, and emerged from this lengthy transformation with improved protection, new machinery and revised armament. She served in the Adriatic during World War I and saw early action against the British Mediterranean Fleet in World War II, being hit by the battleship *Warspite* in the Ionian Sea in July 1940. She was damaged by a near miss in an air raid on Naples in January 1941 and, in December, took part in the Battle of Sirte. In September 1943, she sailed for Malta to surrender to the Allies. At the end of World War II, *Guilio Cesare* was handed over to the Soviet Union and was re-named *Novorossisk*. She served in the Black Sea until 1955.

SPECIFICATIONS

COUNTRY OF ORIGIN: Italy
CREW: 1235
WEIGHT: 29,496 tonnes (29,032 tons)
DIMENSIONS: 186.4m x 28m x 9m (611ft 6in x 92ft x 29ft 6in)
RANGE: 8640km (4800nm) at 10 knots
ARMOUR: 254mm (10in) on sides and turrets
ARMAMENT: 12 x 120mm (4.7in), 10 x 320mm (12.6in) guns
POWERPLANT: quadruple-screw turbines
PERFORMANCE: 28.2 knots

Giuseppe Garibaldi

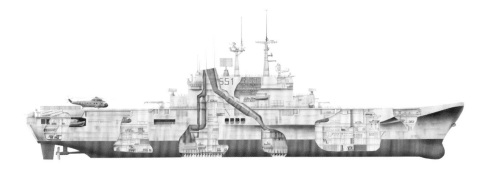

The World War II Peace Treaty banned Italy from having an aircraft carrier, which meant that at the time of launch, *Giuseppe Garibaldi* did not receive its Harriers and was classed as an aircraft-carrying cruiser. The ban was eventually lifted and, in 1989, the Italian Navy obtained fixed-wing aircraft to operate from the ship. *Giuseppe Garibaldi* has six decks with 13 watertight bulkheads. A 'ski-jump' launch ramp is mounted on the bows for vertical take-off and landing aircraft. It carries up to 16 AV-8B Harrier II jump-jets, or 18 Augusta helicopters, or – more often – a combination of both. The ship includes AN/SPS-52C early warning radar, SPS-702 CORA surface search, SPN-749 navigation, SPN-728 approach, RTN-30 and RTN-10X fire control radar. Albatros eight-cell launchers are installed on the roof decks at the forward and stern end of the main island.

SPECIFICATIONS

COUNTRY OF ORIGIN: Italy
CREW: 550 plus 230 air wing
WEIGHT: 13,500 tonnes (13,370 tons)
DIMENSIONS: 180m x 33.4m x 6.7m (590ft 6in x 109ft 6in x 22ft)
RANGE: 13,000km (7000nm) at 20 knots
ARMOUR: unknown
ARMAMENT: 48 x Aspide missiles and 3 x Selex NA 21 systems control, 3 x 40mm–70mm (1.57–2.76in) twin Oto Melara guns; 16 x Harriers or 18 helicopters
POWERPLANT: 4 x General Electric/Avio LM2500 gas turbines providing 61,147kW (82,000hp), 6 x Diesel generators 9.360KW (12.5hp)
PERFORMANCE: 30 knots

Glatton

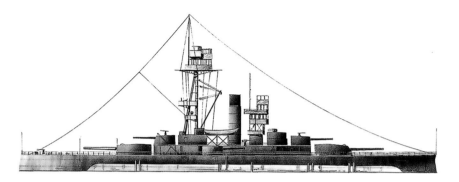

Glatton was one of two coast defence ships ordered by Norway in 1913 and laid down in Britain later that year. In November 1914, both vessels were bought by the Royal Navy for service in World War I and modified to take standard British shells. Due to more pressing building work, Glatton was not completed until 1918. In that year, she was assigned to the Dover patrol, which was intended to prevent German U-boats passing through the English Channel from their North Sea bases. German destroyers from Ostend and Zeebrugge attempted to break down the patrols by sudden raids, but they were repulsed in fierce night actions. Thirteen U-boats were destroyed in the Dover area in 1918. Glatton had been on station for only a short time when she was wrecked by an internal explosion on 16 September 1918, with the loss of 77 crew.

SPECIFICATIONS

COUNTRY OF ORIGIN: United Kingdom
CREW: 305
WEIGHT: 5831 tonnes (5740 tons)
DIMENSIONS: 94.5m x 22.4m x 5m (310ft x 73ft 6in x 16ft 5in)
RANGE: 5003km (2700nm) at 11 knots
ARMOUR: 178–75mm (7–3in) belt, 203mm (8in) on turrets, 203–152mm (8–6in) on barbettes
ARMAMENT: 4 x 152mm (6in), 2 x 233mm (9.2in) guns
POWERPLANT: twin-screw, triple expansion engines
PERFORMANCE: 12 knots

Glorious

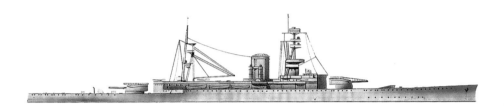

One of the Courageous class of cruisers, *Glorious*, her sister, *Courageous*, and near-sister, *Furious*, combined maximum firepower with speed. Completed in 1917, *Glorious* was laid up in 1919, but, along with her sister ships, she was converted into an aircraft carrier during the 1920s. In the afternoon of 8 June 1940, *Glorious* and her escorts were intercepted by *Scharnhorst* and *Gneisenau*, out on a sortie against the Allied troop transports west of Harstad, Norway. The carrier was caught completely unaware; for reasons that were never explained, none of her reconnaissance Swordfish aircraft were airborne. Desperate attempts were made to arm and launch them as the enemy battlecruisers came in sight, but she was overwhelmed and was sunk before this could be accomplished. Her escorting destroyers, *Ardent* and *Acasta*, were also sunk.

SPECIFICATIONS

COUNTRY OF ORIGIN: United Kingdom
CREW: 842
WEIGHT: 23,327 tonnes (22,960 tons)
DIMENSIONS: 239.5m x 24.7m x 6.7m (785ft 9in x 81ft x 22ft 3in)
RANGE: 5929km (3200nm) at 19 knots
ARMOUR: 76–51mm (3–2in) belt, 228–178mm (9–7in) on turrets
ARMAMENT: 18 x 102mm (4in), 4 x 380mm (15in) guns
POWERPLANT: quadruple-screw, turbines
PERFORMANCE: 33 knots

Gneisenau

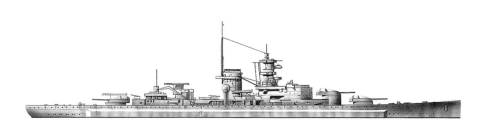

Both launched in 1936, *Gneisenau* and her sister, *Scharnhorst*, were completed with straight stems, but the bows were later lengthened. Both vessels served in World War II, attacking British commerce and sinking the British aircraft carrier *Glorious*. Both ships received damage from air attacks in 1941 while in Brest harbour, and in February 1942, together with the cruiser *Prinz Eugen*, they broke out and made an epic dash across the English Channel, for the north German ports. *Gneisenau* reached Kiel without incident only to be damaged in an RAF bombing raid two weeks later, after which she was moved to Gdynia (Gdansk). She was decommissioned in July 1942 and her turrets were removed for coastal defence. A planned refit was abandoned in 1943 and her hulk was sunk as a blockship at Gdynia in March 1945. Salvaged by the Russians, she was broken up in 1947–51.

SPECIFICATIONS

COUNTRY OF ORIGIN: Germany
CREW: 1840
WEIGHT: 39,522 tonnes (38,900 tons)
DIMENSIONS: 226m x 30m x 9m (741ft 6in x 98ft 5in x 29ft 6in)
RANGE: 16,306km (8800nm) at 18 knots
ARMOUR: 343–168mm (13.75–6.75in) belt, 356–152mm (14–6in) on turrets
ARMAMENT: 14 x 104mm (4.1in), 12 x 150mm (5.9in), 9 x 279mm (11in) guns
POWERPLANT: triple-screw turbines, with diesels for cruising
PERFORMANCE: 32 knots

Goeben

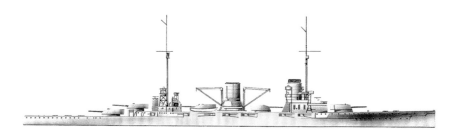

Goeben was one of two ships in the Moltke class that formed the second group of battlecruisers built for the rapidly expanding German Imperial Navy before World War I. With the outbreak of war, *Goeben* and her sister ship, *Breslau*, were pursued across the Mediterranean by British ships *Indomitable* and *Indefatigable*, but they easily outran the British and put into the Turkish port of Constantinople. Both ships were transferred to the Turkish Navy, and *Goeben* was renamed *Yavuz Sultan Selim* on 16 August 1914. In November 1914, she was seriously damaged in action with Russian battleships off Samsoun; in December, she struck two mines on the approaches to the Bosphorus and she was again damaged by Russian warships in May 1915. In January 1918, *Goeben* sank the British monitors Raglan and M28 at Mudros, and was again damaged by mines afterwards. She was broken up in 1954.

SPECIFICATIONS

COUNTRY OF ORIGIN: Germany
CREW: 1053
WEIGHT: 25,704 tonnes (25,300 tons)
DIMENSIONS: 186.5m x 29.5m x 9m (611ft 10in x 96ft 9in x 29ft 6in)
RANGE: 7634km (4120nm) at 14 knots
ARMOUR: 270–100mm (10.7–4in) belt, 229–60mm (9–2.4in) on turrets
ARMAMENT: 12 x 150mm (5.9in), 10 x 280mm (11in) guns
POWERPLANT: quadruple-screw turbines
PERFORMANCE: 28 knots

Graf Spee

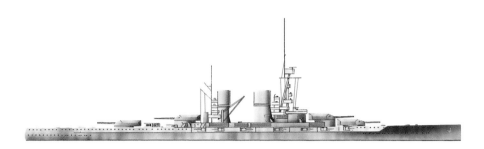

Graf Spee was to have been an improved version of the powerful Hindenburg battlecruiser launched in 1917. The main armament of *Graf Spee* was updated, the weapons being positioned in four twin turrets, two superfiring fore and aft. The secondary armament was concentrated on the upper deck in a long battery that was a continuation of the raised foredeck. The Germans hoped to complete all four vessels in the class by 1918, but although *Graf Spee* was launched in 1917, she was never completed and was scrapped in 1921–23. Other vessels in her class were the *Mackensen*, *Prinz Eitel Friedrich* and *Furst Bismarck*; work on all of these was suspended in 1917 and the last two were never launched. By this time the German Fleet was virtually inactive – except in the Baltic – and materials intended for new-build warships were urgently needed in other sectors of the war industry.

SPECIFICATIONS

COUNTRY OF ORIGIN: Germany
CREW: 1186
WEIGHT: 36,576 tonnes (36,000 tons)
DIMENSIONS: 223m x 30.4m x 8.4m (731ft 8in x 99ft 9in x 27ft 7in)
RANGE: 14,400km (8000nm) at 10 knots
ARMOUR: 300–102mm (11.8–4in) belt and turrets
ARMAMENT: 12 x 150mm (5.9in), 8 x 350mm (13.8in) guns
POWERPLANT: quadruple-screw turbines
PERFORMANCE: 28 knots

Graf Zeppelin

After World War I, Germany was denied any opportunity of developing a carrier force as a result of restrictions imposed upon them in 1919. By 1933, Wilhelm Hadelar had prepared a basic design for a full deck carrier able to operate 40 aircraft, but lack of construction experience delayed the project. In 1935 work began, but *Graf Zeppelin*'s completion was delayed to make way for the U-boat programme. The incomplete carrier was scuttled a few months before the end of World War II. She was raised by the Soviet Union, but sank on her way to Leningrad. *Graf Zeppelin* was originally intended to carry an air group of 12 Ju 87D dive-bombers and 30 Me 109F fighters; this was later amended to 28 Ju 87Ds and 12 Me 109s. Half of a sister ship was also completed. It was speculated that this vessel would be named *Peter Strasser*, after the commander of the German Naval Airship Division in World War I.

SPECIFICATIONS

COUNTRY OF ORIGIN: Germany
CREW: 1760 (estimated)
WEIGHT: 28,540 tonnes (28,090 tons)
DIMENSIONS: 262.5m x 31.5m x 8.5m (861ft 3in x 103ft 4in x 27ft 10in)
RANGE: 14,842km (8000nm) at 19 knots
ARMOUR: 89mm (3.5in) belt, 37.5mm (1.5in) on flight deck
ARMAMENT: 12 x 104mm (4.1in), 16 x 150mm (5.9in) guns, 43 aircraft
POWERPLANT: quadruple-screw turbines
PERFORMANCE: 35 knots

Grosser Kurfürst

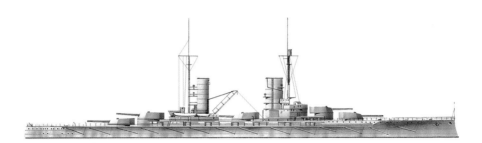

Turbines were used in German battleships for the first time on *Grosser Kurfürst* and her three sisters. The ships were greatly improved versions of *Helgoland*, and had superfiring guns aft, allowing the broadside to be increased from six to ten 305mm (12in) guns. Vessels of this class were contemporaries of the first British 343mm (13.5in) gunned battleships with similar displacement, but where the British had adopted the heavier guns and had only moderate protection, *Grosser Kurfürst* and her sisters retained the 305mm (12in) guns and used more armour. Launched in 1913, *Grosser Kurfürst* saw action at the Battle of Jutland, taking eight hits. She surrendered at the end of World War I and was scuttled with the rest of the German fleet in 1919, before being raised and scrapped in 1934. Her sister ships were *König*, *Kronprinz* and *Markgraf*. Of these, only *König* was not raised after being scuttled.

SPECIFICATIONS

COUNTRY OF ORIGIN: Germany
CREW: 1136
WEIGHT: 28,598 tonnes (28,148 tons)
DIMENSIONS: 175.7m x 29.5m x 8.3m (576ft 5in x 96ft 9in x 27ft 3in)
RANGE: 12,240km (6800nm) at 10 knots
ARMOUR: 350–80mm (14–3.2in) belt, 300–80mm (11.8–3.2in) on turrets
ARMAMENT: 8 x 86mm (3.4in) and 14 x 150mm (5.9in) guns
POWERPLANT: triple-screw turbines
PERFORMANCE: 21 knots

Guam

*G*uam and her sister ship, *Alaska*, were built to combat the fast raiders of the German *Scharnhorst* type, believed in 1940 to be under construction for the Imperial Japanese Navy. *Guam* was an enlarged version of the cruiser *Baltimore*, with three triple turrets housing specially designed 305mm (12in) guns and upgraded armour. Completed in 1944, she was flush-decked, with a single funnel flanked by the cranes for the two catapults which launched the scout planes. Range at 15 knots was 22,800km (12,311nm). In March 1945, she was part of a covering force of warships operating in support of US carriers making a series of air strikes on the Japanese island of Kyushu, and in April–June, she again supported naval task forces attacking Okinawa. Her last operations, in August 1945, were against shipping in the East China Sea. *Guam* was scrapped in 1961.

SPECIFICATIONS

COUNTRY OF ORIGIN: United States
CREW: 1517
WEIGHT: 34,801 tonnes (34,253 tons)
DIMENSIONS: 246m x 27.6m x 9.6m (807ft 5in x 90ft 9in x 31ft 9in)
RANGE: 22,800km (12,000nm) at 15 knots
ARMOUR: 229–127mm (9–5in) belt, 305–203mm (12–8in) on turrets
ARMAMENT: 12 x 127mm (5in), 9 x 305mm (12in) guns
POWERPLANT: quadruple-screw turbines
PERFORMANCE: 33 knots

Habsburg

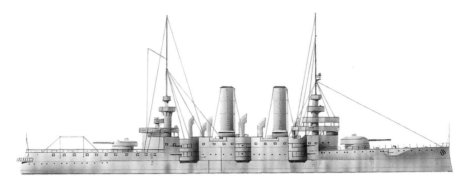

Habsburg was one of a trio of vessels that were the first true Austrian oceangoing battleships since the launching of *Tegetthoff* in 1878. Launched in 1900, she later underwent a reconstruction, having her top superstructure removed in 1910–11. By now, Austria was starting to build new ships at a faster rate, but lack of funds hindered development. However, during the period before World War I, the navy had two staunch supporters, the heir to the throne, Archduke Franz Ferdinand, and the navy commander, Admiral Montecuccoli. It was the latter who ordered Austria's first and only class of Dreadnought in 1911; construction was begun even before the government had actually approved it. After World War I, all three of *Habsburg*'s class (the others being *Arpad* and *Babenberg*) were handed over to Britain and scrapped in 1921.

SPECIFICATIONS

COUNTRY OF ORIGIN: Austria
CREW: 638
WEIGHT: 8964 tonnes (8823 tons)
DIMENSIONS: 114.5m x 19.8m x 7.4m (375ft 8in x 65ft 2in x 24ft 6in)
RANGE: 6670km (3600nm) at 10 knots
ARMOUR: 203–50mm (8–2in) belt, 203–152mm (8–6in) on barbettes and turrets
ARMAMENT: 12 x 150mm (5.9in), 3 x 240mm (9.4in) guns
POWERPLANT: twin-screw, vertical triple expansion engines
PERFORMANCE: 19.6 knots

Haruna

Haruna was one of the first dreadnought-type warships to be laid down in a Japanese yard, and her sister, *Kongo*, was the last major Japanese warship to be built abroad. The four ships in Haruna's class originally had three funnels and light military masts. In 1927–28, *Haruna* underwent a major refit and was reclassified as a battleship. The fore funnel was removed, and the second enlarged and heightened. Sixteen new boilers were installed, bulges were fitted and the armour thickened, increasing the total weight from 6606 tonnes (6502 tons) to 10,478 tonnes (10,313 tons). In December 1941, she formed part of the distant covering force for the Japanese landings in Malaya and the Philippines and then took part in every major action of the Pacific War. *Haruna* was sunk by US aircraft in July 1945. She was raised and broken up in 1946.

SPECIFICATIONS

COUNTRY OF ORIGIN: Japan
CREW: 1221
WEIGHT: 32,715 tonnes (32,200 tons)
DIMENSIONS: 214.5m x 28m x 8.4m (703ft 9in x 91ft 10in x 27ft 6in)
RANGE: 14,400km (8000nm) at 12 knots
ARMOUR: 203–76mm (8–3in) belt, 228mm (9in) on turrets
ARMAMENT: 16 x 152mm (6in), 8 x 355mm (14in) guns
POWERPLANT: quadruple-screw turbines
PERFORMANCE: 27.5 knots

Helgoland

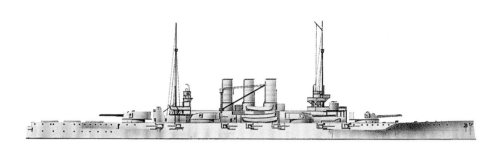

Launched in 1909, *Helgoland* was the last three-funnelled German battleship, and the first to adopt the 304mm (12in) gun as a main armament. All ships in her class served in World War I, two being damaged at the Battle of Jutland in 1916. *Helgoland* herself was hit by one shell. After this decisive battle, the German High Seas Fleet never again contested possession of the North Sea. It sortied on three further occasions, twice in 1916 and once in 1918. None resulted in action, and the low level of activity resulted in disillusionment and, ultimately, open rebellion. The crew of *Helgoland*, in command with most of their compatriots, mutinied in 1918. This turn of events might have been avoided if the High Seas Fleet had embarked on an all-out war against Allied commerce. *Helgoland* was broken up in 1924.

SPECIFICATIONS

COUNTRY OF ORIGIN: Germany
CREW: 1113
WEIGHT: 24,700 tonnes (24,312 tons)
DIMENSIONS: 166.4m x 28.5m x 8.3m (546ft x 93ft 6in x 27ft 6in)
RANGE: 6670km (3600nm) at 18 knots
ARMOUR: 300–102mm (11.8–4in) belt, 280mm (11in) on turrets, 170–75mm (6.7–3in) on casemates
ARMAMENT: 14 x 150mm (5.9in), 12 x 304mm (12in) guns
POWERPLANT: triple-screw, triple expansion engines
PERFORMANCE: 20.3 knots

Henri IV

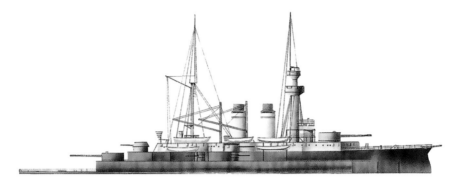

Henri IV was unusual in that weight was saved by cutting down the aft hull leaving very little freeboard. The 270mm (10.8in) guns were carried one forward on the raised superstructure 8.5m (28ft) above the water, and one in the aft turret 4.8m (16ft) above the water. The belt was 2m (7ft) deep, with just over half the depth below the waterline. The decks were flat and armoured. She also had lateral armoured bulkheads. Total weight of armour was about 3556 tonnes (3500 tons). In 1907, Henri IV was damaged off Algiers in a collision with the destroyer Dard, which lost its bow. In March 1915, she was sent to the Dardanelles, where a French naval squadron was operating under the orders of Admiral Carden. She subsequently took part in the bombardment of Turkish forts and, in May, she covered the landing of General Bailloud's Algerian Division. Henri IV was stricken in 1921.

SPECIFICATIONS

COUNTRY OF ORIGIN: France
CREW: 464
WEIGHT: 8948 tonnes (8807 tons)
DIMENSIONS: 108m x 22.2m x 6.9m (354ft 4in x 73ft x 22ft 8in)
RANGE: 11,118km (600nm) at 10 knots
ARMOUR: 254mm (10in) steel plate
ARMAMENT: 7 x 140mm (5.5in), 2 x 274mm (10.8in) guns
POWERPLANT: triple-screw, triple expansion engines
PERFORMANCE: 17 knots

Hermes (1924)

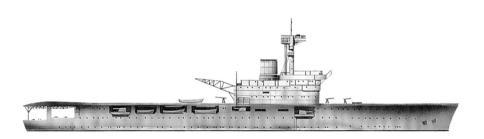

Hermes was the first true purpose-designed aircraft carrier to be ordered by any navy. She was laid down in 1917, but was not completed until 1924, and was thus beaten into service by the Japanese carrier *Hosho*. Her hull had a cruiser form, with the main deck providing the strength. Above this was a 122m (400ft) hangar deck, surmounted by the flight deck. Her bridge, funnel, command centre and masts were all grouped in a large island on the starboard side of the flight deck. Her 150mm (5.9in) guns were set in the hull, while the smaller weapons were mounted on the starboard edge of the flight deck. She could not carry many aircraft and, in 1940, her air wing comprised only 12 fighters. She was sunk by Japanese carrier aircraft off Ceylon on 9 April 1942, together with the Australian destroyer *Vampire*, the corvette *Hollyhock* and two tankers, during an enemy sortie towards Ceylon.

SPECIFICATIONS

COUNTRY OF ORIGIN: United Kingdom
CREW: 664
WEIGHT: 13,208 tonnes (13,000 tons)
DIMENSIONS: 182.9m x 21.4m x 6.5m (600ft 1in x 70ft 2in x 21ft 6in)
RANGE: 7412km (4000nm) at 15 knots
ARMOUR: 5mm (3in) belt, 25mm (1in) deck
ARMAMENT: 3 x 102mm (4in), 6 x 140mm (5.5in) guns
POWERPLANT: twin-screw turbines
PERFORMANCE: 25 knots

Hermes (Viraat)

In 1943, designs were drawn up for a class of eight carriers, with machinery twice as powerful as that installed in the earlier Colossus class. Armour was to be improved, and a stronger flight deck was planned to handle the new, heavier aircraft then entering service. Eventually, only four ships were laid down, and the Admiralty decided to scrap these while they were still on the stocks at the end of World War II. However, due to the inability of many existing carriers to handle the new jet aircraft, construction was continued. After several design changes, *Hermes* was completed in 1959. During a scheduled refit in 1979, she was given a 12-degree ski ramp to operate the British Aerospace Sea Harrier FSR.1 V/STOL strike aircraft, two squadrons of six being embarked. In 1982, she served as flagship during the Falklands War. She was put on reserve in 1984, and later sold to India and relaunched as the INS *Viraat*.

SPECIFICATIONS

COUNTRY OF ORIGIN: United Kingdom
CREW: 1830 and 270 air group
WEIGHT: 25,290 tonnes (24,892 tons)
DIMENSIONS: 224.6m x 30.4m x 8.2m (737ft x 100ft x 27ft)
RANGE: 7412km (4000nm) at 15 knots
ARMOUR: 40mm (1.6in) over magazines, 19mm (0.74in) on flight deck
ARMAMENT: 32 x 40mm (1.6in) guns
POWERPLANT: twin-screw turbines
PERFORMANCE: 29.5 knots

Hood

After the Battle of Jutland in 1916, in which three of Britain's battlecruisers blew up, designs were put in hand for a better-protected vessel. *Hood* was to have been the first of four such ships, but was the only one completed. Her engines developed 147,381kW (144,000hp), and range was 7600km (4104nm) at 10 knots. Despite being designed to avoid the fate of her predecessors, whilst engaging the German battleship *Bismarck* and the cruiser *Prinz Eugen* on 21 May 1941, her upper armour was breached by a shell which reached her magazine, blowing her in two. There were only three survivors, with 1338 were lost. The sinking of *Hood* was keenly felt by the British people, who held her in great affection. She had 'shown the flag' for Britain several times, most notably in 1923, when she embarked on a world cruise. Her assailant, *Bismarck*, survived her by just three days before she too was sunk.

SPECIFICATIONS

COUNTRY OF ORIGIN: United Kingdom
CREW: 1477
WEIGHT: 45,923 tonnes (45,200 tons)
DIMENSIONS: 262m x 31.7m x 8.7m (859ft 7in x 104ft x 28ft 6in)
RANGE: 7200km (4000nm) at 10 knots
ARMOUR: 305–127mm (12–5in) belt and barbettes
ARMAMENT: 12 x 140mm (5.5 in), 8 x 381mm (15in) guns
POWERPLANT: quadruple-screw turbines
PERFORMANCE: 32 knots

Ibuki

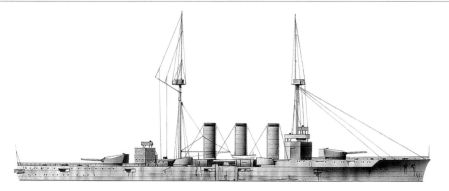

Ibuki was the first Japanese warship to be fitted with turbine engines. Laid down in May 1907, she was quickly built, but her launch was delayed due to other construction work already in hand. The delay enabled her design to be modified, prior to completion, to include the installation of turbine machinery, which developed 17,897kW (24,000hp). Coal supply was 2032 tonnes (2000 tons), plus 221 tonnes (218 tons) of oil fuel. *Ibuki* served as an escort for Australian troops on their way to the Dardanelles during the early part of World War I, and also took part in the search for the German cruiser *Emden*, which was engaged in commerce raiding in the Indian Ocean. *Emden* took 21 Allied ships and also destroyed a small Russian cruiser and a French destroyer, as well as destroying a signal station, before being sunk by the cruiser HMAS *Sydney*. *Ibuki* was scrapped in 1924.

SPECIFICATIONS

COUNTRY OF ORIGIN: Japan
CREW: 844
WEIGHT: 15,844 tonnes (15,595 tons)
DIMENSIONS: 148m x 23m x 8m (485ft 7in x 75ft 4in x 26ft 1in)
RANGE: 6485km (3500nm) at 15 knots
ARMOUR: 178–102mm (7–4in) on belt, barbettes and turrets
ARMAMENT: 4 x 305mm (12in), 8 x 203mm (8in) guns
POWERPLANT: twin-screw turbines
PERFORMANCE: 21 knots

Idaho

Idaho was one of a trio of battleships of the New Mexico class that introduced a new 356mm (14in) gun that could be independently elevated; with previous guns, all weapons in a turret had been locked into the same elevation. The main guns were housed in triple turrets. Originally 22 x 127mm (5in) guns were planned. The number was reduced to 14, allowing extra armour in some areas. Idaho was extensively rebuilt in 1930–31. From 1919 to 1941 she served with the Pacific Fleet, being transferred to the Atlantic Fleet for a brief period before returning to the Pacific. She subsequently fought actions off Attu, the Gilbert Islands, Kwajalein, Saipan, Guam, Palau, Iwo Jima and Okinawa, running aground off the latter island in June 1945. By 1943, she had had all her 127mm (5in) guns removed. Idaho was stricken in 1947; her sister ships were New Mexico and Mississippi.

SPECIFICATIONS

COUNTRY OF ORIGIN: United States
CREW: 1084
WEIGHT: 33,528 tonnes (33,000 tons)
DIMENSIONS: 190.2m x 29.7m x 9.1m (624ft x 97ft 6in x 29ft 10in)
RANGE: 14,400km (8000nm) at 10 knots
ARMOUR: 343–203mm (13.5–8in) belt, 254–229mm (10–9in) on sides, 450mm (18in) on turrets
ARMAMENT: 12 x 356mm (14in), 14 x 127mm (5in) guns
POWERPLANT: quadruple-screw turbines
PERFORMANCE: 21 knots

Imperator Pavel I

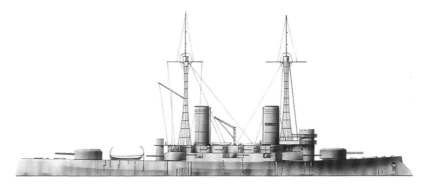

Imperator Pavel I was laid down in April 1904, but construction was delayed to incorporate lessons learned in the Russo-Japanese War of 1904–05. The hull was completely armoured and flush-decked. The superstructure housed six of the 203mm (8in) guns and all of the 12 120mm (4.7in) guns, with twin 203mm (8in) turrets mounted on the upper deck at each corner of the superstructure. The 304mm (12in) guns were in turrets. She saw action in the Baltic during World War I and was renamed Respublika after the successful Russian revolution in 1917. She was scrapped in 1923. The Baltic, where this vessel spent its operational service, was the scene of a number of fierce naval actions during World War I, as the Russians attempted to contest German domination of the Baltic states. Most actions were fought against warships of the German 3rd High Sea Squadron.

SPECIFICATIONS

COUNTRY OF ORIGIN: Russia
CREW: 933
WEIGHT: 17,678 tonnes (17,400 tons)
DIMENSIONS: 140.2m x 24.4m x 8.2m (460ft x 80ft 1in x 27ft)
RANGE: 11,118km (6000nm) at 12 knots
ARMOUR: 127–216mm (5–8.5in) thick belt, 102–203mm (4–8in) on main turrets and 127–165mm (5–6.5in) on battery
ARMAMENT: 4 x 305mm (12in), 14 x 203mm (8in) and 12 x 120mm (4.7in) guns
POWERPLANT: twin-screw, vertical triple expansion engines
PERFORMANCE: 17.5 knots

Independence

During 1942, the US Navy lost four aircraft carriers and, for a time, had only *Enterprise* in the Pacific. The first of the large Essex-class carriers were not expected to enter service until the following year, so plans were put in hand to convert some of the 39 light cruisers of the Cleveland class then under construction. Emergency work was carried out on nine of the vessels and they all entered service in 1943. *Independence* had 45 aircraft, but she had room to 'ferry' up to 100. Her World War II battle honours included raids on the Gilbert Islands, Palau, Leyte, Luzon, Taiwan, Okinawa, the China coast, the Ryukus and the Japanese Home Islands. During the invasion of the Gilbert Islands in November 1943, *Independence* was severely damaged by an aerial torpedo off Tarawa. She was used as a target in the Bikini atomic bomb tests, and was finally sunk as a target ship in 1951.

SPECIFICATIONS

COUNTRY OF ORIGIN: United States
CREW: 1569
WEIGHT: 14,980 tonnes (14,751 tons)
DIMENSIONS: 189.78m x 33.3m x 7.4m (622ft 6in x 109ft 2in x 24ft 3in)
RANGE: 23,400km (13,000nm) at 12 knots
ARMOUR: 127mm (5in) belt and bulkheads, armour: deck 50mm (2in)
ARMAMENT: 2 x 40mm (1.5in), 22 x 20mm (0.78in) guns, 30 x aircraft
POWERPLANT: quadruple-screw turbines
PERFORMANCE: 31.6 knots

Indiana

Indiana was one of a class of four units of the South Dakota class that were the last US battleships designed within the weight limits of the 1922 London Treaty. Completed in 1942, all *Indiana*'s secondary 127mm (5in) guns were concentrated on two levels in twin turrets amidships, and her single funnel was faired into the rear of the bridge. The class carried over 100 40mm (1.5in) and 20mm (0.78in) anti-aircraft guns. *Indiana* saw extensive service in the Pacific during World War II. She saw action in the Southwest Pacific, the Gilbert Islands, Kwajalein, the Philippine Sea, Saipan, Guam, Palau, Iwo Jima and Okinawa. In February 1944, *Indiana* was damaged in collision with the battleship *Washington* off Kwajalein; in June that year she was hit by a suicide aircraft off Saipan; and in June 1945, she was further damaged by a typhoon off Okinawa. She was sold in 1963.

SPECIFICATIONS

COUNTRY OF ORIGIN: United States
CREW: 1793
WEIGHT: 45,231 tonnes (44,519 tons)
DIMENSIONS: 207.2m x 32.9m x 10.6m (679ft 9in x 108ft x 34ft 9in)
RANGE: 27,000km (15,000nm) at 12 knots
ARMOUR: 309mm (12.2in) belt, 457mm (18in) facings on turrets
ARMAMENT: 20 x 127mm (5in), 9 x 406mm (16in) guns
POWERPLANT: quadruple-screw turbines
PERFORMANCE: 27.5 knots

Inflexible

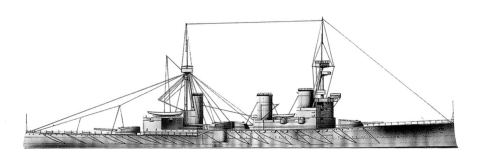

In 1904, the powerful Japanese Tsukuba and Ibuki classes convinced the British Admiralty of the need for a vessel combining the speed of a cruiser with the firepower of a battleship. The answer was *Inflexible* and her sisters of the Invincible class. *Inflexible* was launched in 1907 and completed in 1908. In May 1911, she suffered a damaged bow in collision with the battleship *Bellerophon* in the English Channel. Early in World War I, she took part in the naval action off the Falklands and the hunt for the German cruiser *Goeben*. in 1915, *Inflexible* was one of the vessels covering the Dardanelles landings, and while carrying out a bombardment operation in March she was severely damaged by shore batteries and a mine. She was at Jutland in 1916 but received no damage, unlike her sister *Invincible* which was blown up by German shell fire. *Inflexible* and *Indomitable* were sold for scrap in 1922.

SPECIFICATIONS

COUNTRY OF ORIGIN: United Kingdom
CREW: 784
WEIGHT: 20,320 tonnes (20,000 tons)
DIMENSIONS: 172.8m x 23.9m x 8m (567ft x 78ft 6in x 26ft 10in)
RANGE: 5562km (3090nm) at 10 knots
ARMOUR: 152–102mm (6–4in) belt, 178mm (7in) on turrets
ARMAMENT: 16 x 102mm (4in), 8 x 305mm (12in) guns
POWERPLANT: quadruple-screw turbines
PERFORMANCE: 25.5 knots

Invincible

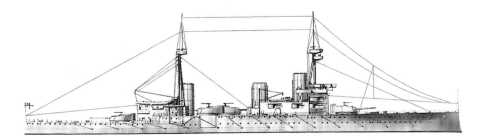

Completed in 1908, *Invincible* was the world's first battlecruiser, and so was the first of an entirely new type of warship. It sacrificed armoured protection for speed, range and battleship-sized armament, and could outrun and outfight its prey, the armoured cruiser. However – as the disastrous loss of *Invincible* and two other battlecruisers at Jutland was to show – when up against a battleship's firepower, the lack of armour, particularly around the magazines, was a fatal flaw. Despite being refitted with more armour as a result of the this débâcle, events had proved the obsolescence of this type of vessel and development was stopped. *Invincible* blew up and sank with the loss of 1026 lives, including Rear Admiral H.L.A. Hood. The battlecruiser *Queen Mary* suffered the same fate at Jutland, exploding with the loss of 1266 lives after a direct hit from the battlecruiser *Derfflinger*.

SPECIFICATIONS

COUNTRY OF ORIGIN: United Kingdom
CREW: 784
WEIGHT: 20,421 tonnes (20,100 tons)
DIMENSIONS: 175.5m x 23.9m x 7.7m (575ft 9in x 78ft 5in x 25ft 3in)
RANGE: 5559km (3000nm) at 25 knots
ARMOUR: 152mm (6in) belt, 178mm (7in) on barbettes and bulkheads
ARMAMENT: 8 x 305mm (12in), 16 x 102mm (4in) guns
POWERPLANT: four-shaft geared turbines
PERFORMANCE: 25 knots

Invincible (CVS)

Commissioned in 1980, *Invincible*'s 70° (later 120°) 'ski-jump' let its Sea Harriers take off at low, fuel-saving speed. It was deployed with the Falkland Islands Task Force in April–June 1982; in the Adriatic Sea during the Yugoslav wars in 1993–95; and off Iraq in 1988–99. *Invincible* was decommissioned in August 2005. The Royal Navy maintained that *Invincible* could be deployed should the need arise. However, work began on breaking up *Invincible* in 2011. The *Invincible* carried up to 15 aircraft, including FA2 Sea Harriers, RAF Harrier GR7, Merlin, Lynx and Sea King helicopters. The aircraft carrier included BAE Systems ADIMP with communication links, multi-function consoles and flat-screen display. The surface search radar antenna was mounted at the top of the main tower.

SPECIFICATIONS

COUNTRY OF ORIGIN: United Kingdom
CREW: 726 plus 384 air wing
WEIGHT: 21,031 tonnes (20,700 tons)
DIMENSIONS: 210m x 36m x 8.8m (689ft x 118ft 1in x 28ft 10in)
RANGE: 13,000km (7000nm) at 18 knots
ARMOUR: unknown
ARMAMENT: Sea Dart anti-air and anti-missile missiles (removed c.1995), Goalkeeper CIWS
POWERPLANT: 4 x Rolls-Royce Olympus TM3B gas turbines providing 72,333kW (97,000hp)
PERFORMANCE: 28 knots

Iowa

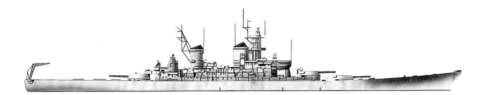

Designs for the Iowa class of fast battleships were started in 1936 in response to rumours that the Japanese were laying down battleships of 46,736 tonnes (46,000 tons). *Iowa* was laid down in 1940 and commissioned in 1943. The class, including the *New Jersey* and *Missouri*, had greater displacement than the previous South Dakota class, and had more power and protection. The Iowa class served as escort for carriers in World War II, being the only battleships fast enough to keep up with carrier groups. *Iowa* was used to bombard shore positions during the Korean War. The last of the Iowas – *Kentucky* – was not launched until 1950. They were the fastest battleships ever built, with a high length to beam ratio; the armour belt was inside the hull. Two of the class, *Illinois* and *Kentucky*, were not completed. *Iowa* was damaged by gunfire from shore batteries on Mili Island in March 1944.

SPECIFICATIONS

COUNTRY OF ORIGIN: United States
CREW: 1921
WEIGHT: 56,601 tonnes (55,710 tons)
DIMENSIONS: 270.4m x 33.5m x 11.6m (887ft 2in x 108ft 3in x 38ft 1in)
RANGE: 27,000km (15,000nm) at 12 knots
ARMOUR: 302–152mm (12.1–6.1in) belt, 152mm (6in) on deck, 492–290mm (19.7–11.6in) on turrets
ARMAMENT: 9 x 406mm (16in), 20 x 127mm (5in) guns
POWERPLANT: quadruple-screw turbines
PERFORMANCE: 32.5 knots

Iron Duke

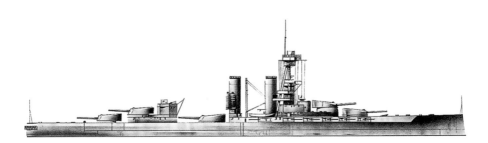

Launched in 1912, *Iron Duke* was the British flagship at the Battle of Jutland in 1916, and was one of the longest serving pre-World War I dreadnought battleships. She was a member of a class of four vessels that formed the third group of super-dreadnoughts. They were all armed with 343mm (13.5in) guns, and were the first major capital ships to revert to 152mm (6in) guns for anti-torpedo boat defence. Minor changes were later made to the secondary armament. The rest of her class was scrapped to comply with the Washington Treaty in the 1920s, but *Iron Duke* herself became a training ship in 1931, and was a depot ship at Scapa Flow between 1939–45. On 17 October 1939, she was attacked by four Junkers Ju88 dive-bombers of I/KG30 while at anchor in Scapa Flow and had to be beached after sustaining damage from near-misses. She was finally scrapped in 1946.

SPECIFICATIONS

COUNTRY OF ORIGIN: United Kingdom
CREW: 1022
WEIGHT: 30,866 tonnes (30,380 tons)
DIMENSIONS: 189.8m x 27.4m x 9m (622ft 9in x 90ft x 29ft 6in)
RANGE: 14,000km (7780nm) at 10 knots
ARMOUR: 304–102mm belt (12–4in), 228mm (9in) middle belt, 152–51mm (2–6in) on battery
ARMAMENT: 12 x 152mm (6in), 10 x 342mm (13.5in) guns
POWERPLANT: quadruple-screw turbines
PERFORMANCE: 21.6 knots

Ise

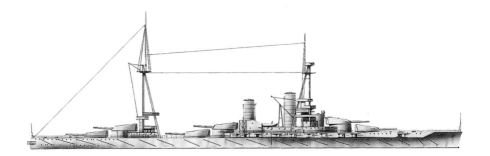

Launched in 1916, *Ise* was an improved version of the previous Fuso class, and carried two twin superfiring guns amidships. She was extensively modernised between World War I and II and, by 1937, had been lengthened aft by 7.6m (25ft). Following the large loss of Japanese aircraft carriers at Midway in June 1942, *Ise* was converted to a hybrid battleship-carrier in 1943 when a hangar and flight deck were built on her quarter deck. Because of a lack of space, her complement of 22 seaplanes were launched by catapult but had to be retrieved by crane. *Ise* took part in the battles of Midway and Leyte Gulf, and was deactivated after being damaged by mines laid by American aircraft. She was sunk at Kure in July 1945 in a two-day series of air strikes that also destroyed the battleships *Hyuga* and *Haruna* and the aircraft carrier *Amagi*. She was raised and scrapped in 1946.

SPECIFICATIONS

COUNTRY OF ORIGIN: Japan
CREW: 1376 as battleship, 1463 as carrier
WEIGHT: 32,576 tonnes (32,063 tons) as battleship
DIMENSIONS: 208.2m x 28.6m x 8.8m (683ft 1in x 94ft x 29ft)
RANGE: 7412km (4000nm) at 15 knots
ARMOUR: 304–229mm (12–9in) belt, 304mm (12in)
ARMAMENT: 12 x 356mm (14in), 20 x 140mm (5.5in) guns
POWERPLANT: quadruple-screw turbines
PERFORMANCE: 23 knots

Iwo Jima

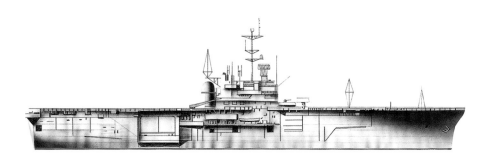

Iwo Jima – first of a class of seven – was the world's first ship designed to carry and operate helicopters. She can also carry a Marine battalion of 2000 troops, plus their artillery and support vehicles. The flight deck allows for the simultaneous take-off of up to seven helicopters, and *Iwo Jima* has hangar facilities for up to 20 helicopters. The two lifts are situated at the very edges of the deck, so as not to reduce the flight-deck area. Storage capacity is provided for 1430 litres (6500 gal) of petrol for the vehicles, plus over 88,000 litres (400,000 gal) for the helicopter force. In 1970, a Sea Sparrow missile launcher was installed, followed by a second three years later. *Iwo Jima* and her six sisters have extensive medical facilities, including operating theatres and a large hospital. Other vessels in the class are *Guadalcanal*, *Guam*, *Inchon*, *Okinawa*, *Tripoli* and *New Orleans*.

SPECIFICATIONS

COUNTRY OF ORIGIN: United States
CREW: 667, plus 2000 troops
WEIGHT: 18,330 tonnes (18,042 tons)
DIMENSIONS: 183.6m x 25.7m x 8m (602ft 8in x 84ft 4in x 26ft 3in)
RANGE: 11,118km (6000nm) at 18 knots
ARMOUR: 100mm (2in) flight deck, 200mm (4in) belt
ARMAMENT: 4 x 76mm (3in) guns
POWERPLANT: single-screw turbines
PERFORMANCE: 23.5 knots

Jeanne D'Arc

Originally to be named *La Résolue*, this ship was authorized in 1957 as a training cruiser to replace the pre-World War I *Jeanne D'Arc*. Due to the cancellation of a large carrier, *La Résolue* underwent major design changes, emerging in 1964 as *Jeanne D'Arc*, a combination of cruiser, helicopter carrier and assault ship. Her superstructure is situated forward, with the aft of the vessel being a helicopter deck below which is housed the narrow hangar. In her role as a troop carrier, *Jeanne D'Arc* can transport 700 men and eight large helicopters. In 1975, Exocet missiles were fitted, giving her a full anti-ship role. In peacetime she reverts to a training role, providing facilities for up to 198 cadets. The ship has a modular type action information and operations room with a computerized tactical data handling system, and a combined command and control centre for amphibious warfare operations.

SPECIFICATIONS

COUNTRY OF ORIGIN: France
CREW: 627, plus 198 cadets
WEIGHT: 13,208 tonnes (13,000 tons)
DIMENSIONS: 180m x 25.9m x 6.2m (590ft 6in x 85ft x 20ft 4in)
RANGE: 10,800km (6000nm) at 12 knots
ARMOUR: classified
ARMAMENT: 4 x 100mm (3.9in) guns, Exocet missiles, 48 helicopters
POWERPLANT: twin-screw turbines
PERFORMANCE: 26.5 knots

Kaiser

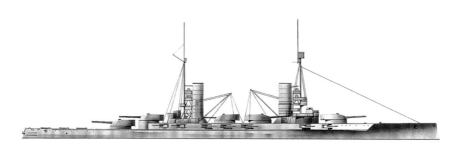

Launched in 1911 and completed in 1912, *Kaiser* was the first of a new type of German dreadnought that was to set the style for following vessels and eventually develop into *Bismarck* and *Tirpitz* of World War II. There were five units in the Kaiser class. All had superfiring turrets aft and diagonally offset wing turrets. Machinery developed 23,117kW (31,000hp), coal supply was 3000 tonnes (2953 tons), and range at 12 knots was nearly 15,200km (8207nm). *Kaiser* was in action at the Battle of Jutland, and all vessels in the class were interned at Scapa Flow and scuttled in 1919. From 1929–37 the class was salvaged and broken up. *Kaiser* was originally laid down as *Ersatz Hildebrand*. Other vessels in her class were *Friedrich der Grosse*, *Kaiserin*, *König Albert* and *Prinzregent Luitpold*. They were the first German battleships to be equipped with turbines.

SPECIFICATIONS

COUNTRY OF ORIGIN: Germany
CREW: 1278 (at Jutland)
WEIGHT: 26,998 tonnes (26,573 tons)
DIMENSIONS: 172.4m x 29m x 8.3m (565ft 8in x 95ft 2in x 27ft 3in)
RANGE: 15,200km (8000nm) at 12 knots
ARMOUR: 350–80mm (14–3.2in) belt and turrets
ARMAMENT: 10 x 304mm (12in), 14 x 150mm (5.9in) guns
POWERPLANT: triple-screw turbines
PERFORMANCE: 23.5 knots

Kiev

Kiev was the first Soviet aircraft carrier to be built with a full flight deck and a purpose-built hull. She was laid down in September 1970 in the Black Sea Nikolayev Dockyard and was completed in May 1975. The flight deck was angled, with most of the armament carried forward, comprising a full range of anti-ship, anti-air and anti-submarine missiles. Twenty-four of the lethal SS-N-12 Shaddock type missiles were carried. The large bridge structure was set on *Kiev*'s starboard side, and housed an array of radar equipment. Designated a 'through-deck cruiser' by the Russians, the ship sailed from the Black Sea in the summer of 1976, passed through the Mediterranean and joined the Soviet Northern Fleet. *Kiev* carried an air group of Yakovlev Yak-38 Forger VTOL fighter-bombers and anti-submarine helicopters. Other vessels in the Kiev class were *Minsk*, *Novorossiysk* and *Baku*.

SPECIFICATIONS

COUNTRY OF ORIGIN: Soviet Union
CREW: 1700
WEIGHT: 38,608 tonnes (38,000 tons)
DIMENSIONS: 273m x 47.2m x 8.2m (895ft 8in x 154ft 10in x 27ft)
RANGE: 24,300km (13,500nm)
ARMOUR: 100mm (4in) flight deck, 50mm (2in) belt
ARMAMENT: 4 x 76.2mm (3in) guns, plus up to 136 missiles
POWERPLANT: quadruple-screw turbines
PERFORMANCE: 32 knots

King Edward VII

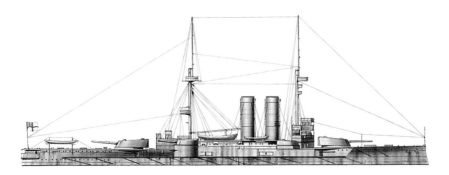

King Edward VII has the historical distinction of being the first British battleship built in the 20th century. She was laid down in 1902, completed three years later, and was first in a class of eight. Known throughout the service for her eccentric steering, she also suffered in having a mixed secondary armament, which prevented her employing large enough weapons in high enough numbers. *King Edward VII* hit a German mine off northern Scotland in 1916 and sank after a 12-hour struggle. Other ships in this class were *Africa*, *Britannia*, *Commonwealth*, *Dominion*, *Hibernia*, *Hindustan* and *New Zealand*. In 1912, *Hibernia* was fitted with a flying-off platform, and on 9 May 1912, Lt C.R. Samson became the first pilot in the world to take off in an aircraft from a ship under way, flying a Short seaplane off the platform as *Hibernia* steamed into wing at 10kt.

SPECIFICATIONS

COUNTRY OF ORIGIN: United Kingdom
CREW: 777
WEIGHT: 17,566 tonnes (17,290 tons)
DIMENSIONS: 138.3m x 23.8m x 7.72m (453ft 9in x 78ft 1in x 25ft 8in)
RANGE: 12,970km (7000nm) at 10 knots
ARMOUR: 229–203mm (9–8in) belt, 305mm (12in) on barbettes, 304–203mm (12–8in) on gun houses
ARMAMENT: 4 x 304mm (12in), 4 x 230mm (9.2in) guns
POWERPLANT: twin-shaft vertical triple expansion engine
PERFORMANCE: 18.5 knots

Kirishima

Launched in 1913 as a Kongo class battlecruiser, *Kirishima* underwent reconstruction between 1927–30 and, like the rest of the class, was reclassified as a battleship. Further rebuilding between 1934–36 completely altered her aft, added over 393 tonnes (400 tons) of armour to her barbettes and increased her anti-aircraft armament. In December 1941, *Kirishima* was part of the escort to the carriers whose aircraft attacked Pearl Harbor; she subsequently covered Japanese landings at Rabaul and in the Dutch East Indies and, on 1 March 1942, she sank the destroyer USS *Edsall* south of Java. During the second Battle of Guadalcanal in November 1942, *Kirishima* fell victim to the accurate radar-directed gunfire of USS *Washington*. At night, over a range of 76.7km (41nm), she was hit by nine 400mm (16in) and 40 127mm (5in) shells and had to be scuttled.

SPECIFICATIONS

COUNTRY OF ORIGIN: Japan
CREW: 1437 (after 1936 re-fit)
WEIGHT: 32,491 tonnes (31,980 tons) as battleship
DIMENSIONS: 219.6m x 222.1m x 9.7m (720ft 6in x 738ft 7in x 31ft 11in)
RANGE: 14,824km (8000nm) at 14 knots
ARMOUR: 203–75mm (8–3in), 254mm (10in) on barbettes, 229mm (9in) on turrets
ARMAMENT: 8 x 356mm (14in), 14 x 152mm (6in), 8 x 127mm (5in) guns
POWERPLANT: four-shaft turbines
PERFORMANCE: 30.4 knots

K

Kniaz Suvarov

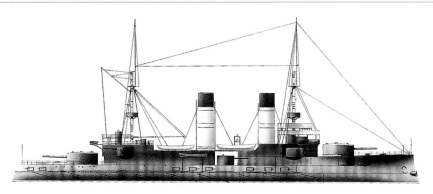

Launched in 1902 and completed in September 1904, *Kniaz Suvarov* was the Russian flagship at the Battle of Tsushima in May 1905, and was sunk by Japanese torpedoes. She was one of five vessels of the Borodino class. Her sister ships, *Borodino* and *Alexander*, were also sunk at Tsushima, while *Orel* surrendered to Japanese forces, later being renamed *Iwami*. The remaining ship in the class, *Slavia*, was not completed in time to join her ill-fated sisters. While en route to their fatal rendezvous, the Russian ships created a major diplomatic incident by opening fire on some British trawlers (which the crews mistook for Japanese torpedo boats) in the North Sea. Gibraltar was put on a war footing and 28 British warships stood ready to intercept and destroy the Russian Pacific Squadron for several hours before the situation was defused.

SPECIFICATIONS

COUNTRY OF ORIGIN: Russia
CREW: 835
WEIGHT: 13,730 tonnes (13,513 tons)
DIMENSIONS: 121m x 23m x 7.9m (397ft x 76ft 2in x 26ft 2in)
RANGE: 12,274km (6624nm) at 10 knots
ARMOUR: 190–152mm (7.5–6in) belt, 254–102mm (10–4in) on turrets
ARMAMENT: 12 x 152mm (6in), 4 x 304mm (12in), 20 x 11-pounder guns
POWERPLANT: twin-screw, vertical triple expansion engines
PERFORMANCE: 17.5 knots

Kongo

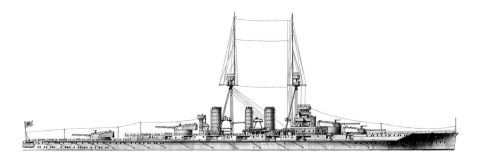

Completed in 1912, *Kongo* and her sisters, *Hiei*, *Haruna* and *Kirishima*, were inspired by the design and performance of British battlecruisers, *Kongo* herself being built in a British yard. Following the lessons of World War I and the naval treaties of the 1930s, the class was rebuilt with greater deck armour and anti-torpedo bulges. The development of fast carrier groups also led to further remodelling, including an improvement of machinery which took the speed of the class up to 30 knots. All four vessels were sunk during World War II. *Kongo* was torpedoed by the US submarine *Sealion* in November 1944. Of the others, *Hiei* and *Kirishima* were both sunk in the battle for Guadalcanal, the former receiving 50 shell hits, one bomb hit from a B-17, and two torpedo hits from aircraft operating from the USS *Enterprise*. *Haruna* was sunk by US aircraft at Kure in July 1945.

SPECIFICATIONS

COUNTRY OF ORIGIN: Japan
CREW: 1221
WEIGHT: 27,940 tonnes (27,500 tons)
DIMENSIONS: 214.7m x 28m x 8.4m (704ft 5in x 92ft x 27ft 7in)
RANGE: 14,824km (8000nm) at 14 knots
ARMOUR: 203mm (8in) belt, 254mm (10in) on barbettes
ARMAMENT: 8 x 356mm (14in), 16 x 152mm (6in) guns
POWERPLANT: four-shaft, geared turbines
PERFORMANCE: 27.5 knots

Leonardo da Vinci

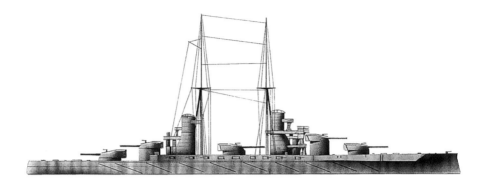

Leonardo da Vinci and her two sisters were an improvement on the previous *Dante Alighieri* class, having 13 big guns mounted in five centreline turrets, with superfiring twin turrets fore and aft. Instead of carrying the secondary armament in twin turrets, the battery was concentrated amidships in casemates. Machinery developed 23,117kW (31,000hp), and range at 10 knots was 8640km (4800 miles). *Leonardo da Vinci* was completed in 1914, and spent her war service in the Adriatic. On 2 August 1916, she caught fire, blew up and capsized at Taranto. The explosion, which was caused either by unstable cordite or Austrian sabotage, left 249 dead. In September 1919, she was refloated upside down and was righted in January 1921. However, she was not repaired and was broken up in 1923. Her two sister ships were *Conte de Cavour* and *Giulio Cesare*.

SPECIFICATIONS

COUNTRY OF ORIGIN: Italy
CREW: 1235
WEIGHT: 25,250 tonnes (25,086 tons)
DIMENSIONS: 176m x 28m x 9.3m (577ft 9in x 91ft 10in x 30ft 10in)
RANGE: 8640km (4800nm) at 10 knots
ARMOUR: 248–127mm (9.8–5in) belt, 280mm (11in) on turrets, 127–110mm (5–4.3in) on secondary battery
ARMAMENT: 13 x 304mm (12in), 18 x 120mm (4.7in) guns
POWERPLANT: quadruple-screw turbines
PERFORMANCE: 21.6 knots

Lexington

Lexington was the first fleet aircraft carrier completed for the US Navy. She was laid down in 1921 as a battlecruiser, but work was stopped as a result of the 1922 Washington Naval Treaty. Her design was then changed to that of an aircraft carrier, though her cruiser-type hull form was retained. A 137m x 21m (450ft x 69ft) hangar was installed and for many years she remained the largest aircraft carrier afloat. In May 1942, Lexington was operating as part of Task Force 11, one of three Allied naval task forces which combined to thwart a Japanese landing at Port Moresby, New Guinea, in the Battle of the Coral Sea. On the morning of 8 May, the opposing carrier forces sighted one another and flew off their aircraft (90 Japanese and 78 American) to attack. Lexington (under Capt F.C. Sherman) was hit by two torpedoes and three bombs and was abandoned, being sunk later by the destroyer USS Phelps.

SPECIFICATIONS

COUNTRY OF ORIGIN: United States
CREW: 2327
WEIGHT: 48,463 tonnes (47,700 tons)
DIMENSIONS: 270.6m x 32.2m x 9.9m (887ft 9in x 105ft 8in x 32ft 6in)
RANGE: 18,900km (10,500nm) at 10 knots
ARMOUR: 178–127mm (7–5in) belt, 31mm (1.2in) on armoured deck
ARMAMENT: 8 x 203mm (8in), 12 x 127mm (5in) guns, 80 x aircraft
POWERPLANT: quadruple-screw turbo electric drive
PERFORMANCE: 33.2 knots

Lion

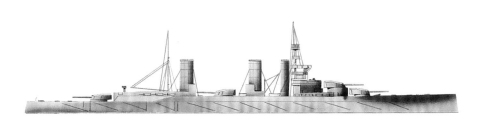

The Lion class of ship were the first battlecruisers to surpass battleships in terms of size. Launched in 1910 and completed in 1912, *Lion* had eight 343mm (13.5in) guns. These were mounted in twin turrets, two forward with one superfiring, one aft and one amidships (the latter having a restricted arc of fire) between the second and third funnels. During World War I, *Lion* was the flagship of the Grand Fleet's Battlecruiser Fleet (commanded by Adm Sir David Beatty). On 24 January 1915, *Lion* received a total of 21 shell hits during the Battle of Dogger Bank and, during the Battle of Jutland in 1916, she narrowly escaped destruction when she was severely damaged by 12 shells, with the loss of 99 of her crew. She was eventually sold and broken up at Blyth, Northumberland, in 1924.

SPECIFICATIONS

COUNTRY OF ORIGIN: United Kingdom
CREW: 997
WEIGHT: 30,154 tonnes (29,680 tons)
DIMENSIONS: 213.3m x 27m x 8.7m (700ft x 88ft 6in x 28ft 10in)
RANGE: 10,098km (5610nm) at 10 knots
ARMOUR: 127–228mm (5–9in) main belt, 102–152mm (46in) upper belt, 102–228mm (4–9in) on turrets
ARMAMENT: 16 x 102mm (4.2in), 8 x 343mm (13.5in) guns
POWERPLANT: quadruple-screw turbines
PERFORMANCE: 27 knots

Littorio

Littorio was one of the last battleships to be built for the Italian Navy. Completed in 1940, she was also the first Italian battleship to be commissioned after World War I. Her impressive outline was all the more striking due to the raised height of the aft turret, which was designed to avoid blast damage to the two fighter planes carried on the poop deck. On 12 November 1940, Littorio was severely damaged by three torpedoes dropped by Swordfish aircraft during the Royal Navy's attack on Taranto, and she received further damage in June 1942 when she was torpedoed by British aircraft during an attack on a Malta convoy. In 1943, she was renamed *Italia*, and after the Italian surrender she was damaged by a German radio-controlled bomb. She was interned on the Suez Canal's Great Bitter Lake until February 1946. Stricken in 1948, she was broken up in 1960.

SPECIFICATIONS

COUNTRY OF ORIGIN: Italy
CREW: 1950
WEIGHT: 46,698 tonnes (45,963 tons)
DIMENSIONS: 237.8m x 32.9m x 9.6m (780ft 2in x 108ft x 31ft 6in)
RANGE: 8487km (4580nm) at 16 knots
ARMOUR: 280–70mm (10.9–2.7in), 350–280mm (13.6–10.9in) on barbettes, 350–200mm (12–7.8in) on turrets
ARMAMENT: 9 x 380mm (15in), 12 x 152mm (6in), 4 x 120mm (4.7in) 11 x 89mm (3.5in) guns
POWERPLANT: quadruple-screw turbines
PERFORMANCE: 28 knots

Lord Nelson

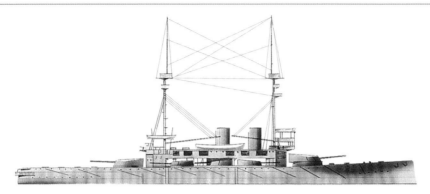

L ord Nelson and her sister, Agamemnon, were the last pre-dreadnoughts built for the Royal Navy. Lord Nelson was completed in October 1908. The 305mm (12in) guns were in twin turrets, with the 233mm (9.2in) guns in a mix of twin and single turrets on the broadside. The main belt ran her full length, supplemented by an upper belt which ran to the base of the 'Y' turret. Lord Nelson was further protected by a number of solid bulkheads, the first to be fitted to a British battleship. She saw extensive service during World War I, a notable action being the bombardment of the Narrows at the Dardanelles on 7 March 1915. Lord Nelson and Agamemnon had engaged Turkish forts with direct gunfire at a range of 11–13km (6–7nm), putting two forts out of action. The British ships were covered by the French battleships Gaulois, Charlemagne, Bouvet and Suffren. Lord Nelson was broken up in 1920.

SPECIFICATIONS

COUNTRY OF ORIGIN: United Kingdom
CREW: 900
WEIGHT: 17,945 tonnes (17,663 tons)
DIMENSIONS: 135m x 24m x 7.9m (443ft 6in x 79ft 6in x 26ft)
RANGE: 17,010km (9180nm) at 10 knots
ARMOUR: 304–203mm (12–8in) belt, 203–178mm (8–7in) on turrets
ARMAMENT: 4 x 304mm (12in), 10 x 233mm (9.2in) guns
POWERPLANT: twin-screw, triple expansion engines
PERFORMANCE: 18.7 knots

Michigan

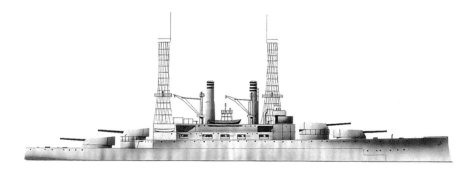

Completed in 1910, *Michigan* was designed before, but built after, the epoch-making Dreadnought class. One of the South Carolina class, her design introduced the concept of all-big-guns on the centreline. Most of the 76mm (3in) guns were concentrated in a box battery amidships, with the rest on the upper deck. Cage masts greatly reduced the target area offered to enemy gunners and were a characteristic of US dreadnoughts. As the turbine was still in the development stage, triple expansion engines were installed instead. *Michigan* served with the Atlantic Fleet between 1910 and 1916 and, in 1917–18, was employed on convoy escort duty. In January 1918, she lost her cage foremast in a storm off Cape Hatteras, and in 1919 she made two voyages as a troop transport, bringing US servicemen home from Europe. She was decommissioned in 1922 and broken up at Philadelphia in 1924.

SPECIFICATIONS

COUNTRY OF ORIGIN: United States
CREW: 869
WEIGHT: 18,186 tonnes (17,900 tons)
DIMENSIONS: 138.2m x 24.5m x 7.5m (453ft 5in x 80ft 4in x 24ft 7in)
RANGE: 9000km (5000nm) at 10 knots
ARMOUR: 304–229mm (12–9in) belt, 304–203mm (12–8in) on turrets
ARMAMENT: 8 x 305mm (12in), 22 x 76mm (3in) guns
POWERPLANT: twin screw, vertical triple expansion engines
PERFORMANCE: 18.5 knots

Minas Gerais

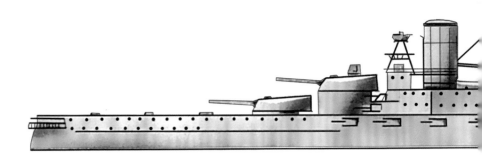

Minas Gerais was originally designed as a pre-dreadnought battleship in answer to the powerful vessels then being built for Chile. Her design was later modified and she became the first powerful dreadnought to be built for a minor navy. She was constructed in Britain and completed in 1910. She was extensively modernised in the US in 1923, and again in Brazil from 1934 to 1937. Minas Gerais was scrapped in 1954. Brazil offered the services of both ships of this class (the other being Sao Paulo) for service with the British Grand Fleet in 1917, after the country revoked its neutrality and seized German ships in Brazilian ports, but the offer was declined because of fuel problems. Tentative plans for Brazilian warships to serve in European waters in 1918 under the command of Adm Bonti did not materialise.

SPECIFICATIONS

COUNTRY OF ORIGIN: Brazil
CREW: 900
WEIGHT: 21,540 tonnes (21,200 tons)
DIMENSIONS: 165.8m x 25.3m x 8.5m (544ft x 83ft x 27ft 10in)
RANGE: 18,000km (10,000nm) at 10 knots
ARMOUR: 229mm (9in) belt, 304–229mm (12–9in) on turrets

ARMAMENT: 12 x 304mm (12in), 22 x 120mm (4.7in) guns
POWERPLANT: twin-screw, vertical triple reciprocating engines
PERFORMANCE: 21 knots

Mikasa

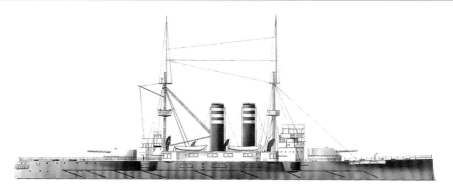

Completed in 1902, *Mikasa* was the last battleship built under the Japanese naval expansion programme of 1896, and was the flagship of Vice-Adm Togo during the Russo-Japanese War of 1904–05. In February 1904, she was hit three times during the bombardment of Port Arthur and, in August, she was again damaged by gunfire in the Battle of the Yellow Sea, receiving 22 hits. *Mikasa* took yet more serious damage at the Battle of Tsushinma on 27 May 1905, when she was hit 32 times. On 12 September that year, she sank at her moorings at Sasebo after an ammunition explosion in her after magazine that left 114 crew dead, but was refloated and recommissioned in August 1906. In 1921, she was reclassified as a coastal defence ship. *Mikasa* retired in 1923 after running aground, and is now on permanent public display as the last surviving battleship of her period.

SPECIFICATIONS

COUNTRY OF ORIGIN: Japan
CREW: 830
WEIGHT: 15,422 tonnes (15,179 tons)
DIMENSIONS: 131.7m x 23.2m x 8.2m (432ft 1in x 76ft 3in x 27ft 2in)
RANGE: 16,677km (9000nm) at 10 knots
ARMOUR: 229–102mm (9–4in) belt, 75–50mm (3–2in) on deck, 356–203mm (14–8in) on turrets
ARMAMENT: 4 x 305mm (12in), 14 x 152mm (6in) guns
POWERPLANT: twin-screw, vertical triple expansion engines
PERFORMANCE: 18 knots

Moltke

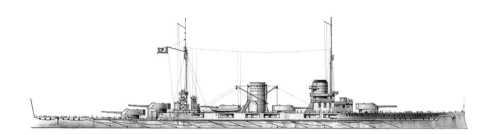

Moltke was laid down in 1909 and completed in 1911 and, like her sister *Goeben*, was the successor to the battlecruiser *Von der Tann*, having two more 280mm (11.1in) guns in a second aft turret. *Moltke* served with Adm Hipper's squadron in World War I and had a remarkable war, surviving two torpedo strikes from British submarines as well as 304mm (12in) shell hits at Jutland. She saw action at Dogger Bank and the Heligoland Bight and took part in the bombardment of English east coast towns. The bombardment of these 'soft' targets, which took place at intervals between November 1914 and the spring of 1916, caused much outrage among the British public, and added to the wealth of stories about German atrocities of the time. *Moltke* was torpedoed by the British submarine E42 but survived. In 1919 she was scuttled with the rest of the German fleet. She was raised and scrapped in 1927.

SPECIFICATIONS

COUNTRY OF ORIGIN: Germany
CREW: 1355 (at Jutland)
WEIGHT: 25,704 tonnes (25,300 tons)
DIMENSIONS: 186.5m x 29.5m x 9m (611ft 11in x 96ft 10in x 26ft 11in)
RANGE: 7416km (4120nm) at 12 knots
ARMOUR: 270–102mm (10.7–4in) belt, 230–30mm (8.9–1.1in) on barbettes, 230mm (8.9in) on turrets
ARMAMENT: 10 x 280mm (11.1in), 12 x 150mm (5.9in) guns
POWERPLANT: four-shaft geared turbines
PERFORMANCE: 28 knots

M

Monarch

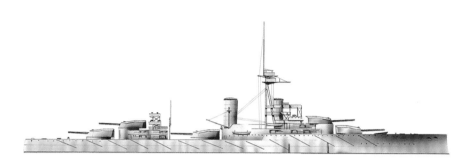

Monarch was one of four units that were the first vessels to carry 343mm (13.5in) guns since the days of the Royal Sovereign class of 1889. With a massive increase of 2540 tonnes (2500 tons) displacement over contemporary dreadnoughts, *Monarch* and her three sisters of the Orion class were called 'superdreadnoughts'. They were the first capital ships of the dreadnought era to carry all the main guns on the centreline. Armour protection was thorough, the side armour rising to upper deck level 5m (17ft) above the waterline. All ships in the class served at Jutland in 1916. *Monarch* was sunk as a target in 1925. Of the other three, *Conqueror* (damaged in a collision with *Monarch* in December 1914) was broken up at Upnor, Kent in December 1922, as was *Orion*; *Thunderer*, which ended her career as a seagoing cadet training ship, was broken up at Blyth in 1924.

SPECIFICATIONS

COUNTRY OF ORIGIN: United Kingdom
CREW: 752
WEIGHT: 26,284 tonnes (25,870 tons)
DIMENSIONS: 177m x 26.9m x 8.7m (580ft 8in x 88ft 6in x 28ft 9in)
RANGE: 12,114km (6730nm) at 10 knots
ARMOUR: 304–203mm (12–8in) belt, 280mm (11in) on turrets
ARMAMENT: 10 x 343mm (13.5in), 16 x 102mm (4in) guns
POWERPLANT: quadruple-screw turbines
PERFORMANCE: 20.8 knots

Moreno

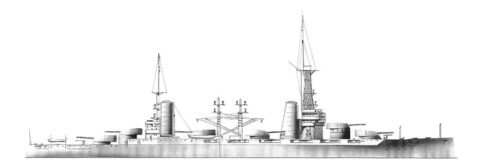

Rivalry between South American republics reached a new height around 1910, when Brazil ordered two powerful dreadnoughts from British yards. Argentina answered with a programme of three dreadnoughts, but owing to financial limitations, only two were ordered, from US yards. *Moreno* and her sister, *Rivadavia*, were modernised in 1924–25. They were converted to run on oil, the lattice mast forward was shortened and the pole mast aft was replaced by a tripod. Displacement increased by 1016 tonnes (1000 tons). In 1937, *Moreno* went on a cruise to Europe, and after service in territorial waters in World War II she successively became a depot ship and a prison ship. Together with her sister ship, *Rivadavia* (which accompanied *Moreno* on her European cruise) she remained Argentina's largest warship until the 1950s. *Moreno* was sold in 1956.

SPECIFICATIONS

COUNTRY OF ORIGIN: Argentina
CREW: 1130
WEIGHT: 30,500 tonnes (30,000 tons)
DIMENSIONS: 173.8m x 29.4m x 8.5m (270ft 3in x 96ft 9in x 27ft 10in)
RANGE: 19,800km (11,000nm) at 12 knots
ARMOUR: 304–254mm (12–10in) belt, 304mm (12in) on turrets
ARMAMENT: 12 x 304mm (12in), 12 x 152mm (6in), guns
POWERPLANT: threeshaft geared turbines
PERFORMANCE: 22.5 knots

Moskva

Moskva was the first helicopter carrier built for the Soviet Navy. She was laid down in 1962 and completed in 1967. She was designed to counter-act the growing threat from the US nuclear-powered missile submarines that first entered service in 1960, and to undertake search and destroy missions. However, by the time *Moskva* and *Leningrad* had been completed at the Nikolayev South shipyard, they were incable of coping with both the numbers and capabilities of NATO submarines, so the building programme was terminated. Classed by the Russians as PKR (Protivolodochnyy Kreyser, or anti-submarine cruiser) the ships proved to be poor sea boats in heavy weather. *Moskva* had a massive central block which dominated the vessel and housed the major weapons systems and a huge sonar array. She was scrapped in the late 1990s.

SPECIFICATIONS

COUNTRY OF ORIGIN: Soviet Union
CREW: 850
WEIGHT: 14,800 tonnes (14,567 tons)
DIMENSIONS: 191m x 34m x 7.6m (626ft 8in x 111ft 6in x 25ft)
RANGE: 8100km (4500nm) at 12 knots
ARMOUR: 102mm (4in) deck, 51mm (2in) superstructure
ARMAMENT: 1 x twin SUW-N-1 launcher, 2 x twin SA-N-3 missile launchers, 1420 x helicopters
POWERPLANT: twin-screw turbines
PERFORMANCE: 30 knots

Nagato

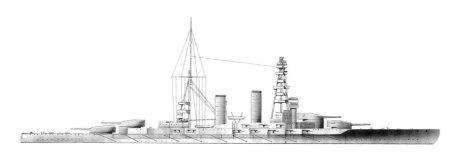

Nagato and her sister, *Mutsu*, heralded a new era in battleship design with the adoption of the 406mm (16in) gun. Completed in 1920, it had a range of some 40km (25 miles), combining great accuracy with greater destructive power. A massive tripod foremast rose above a large bridge structure and, in the mid-1920s, the first funnel was angled back to clear the bridge and mast of smoke fumes. New machinery requiring only one funnel was installed between 1934 and 1936, and the first funnel was then removed. As flagship of the Combined Fleet, *Nagato* saw action at Midway and in the Battle of the Philippine Sea. In October 1944, she received bomb damage at Leyte Gulf and was out of action for the remainder of the war at Yokosuka. In July 1946, *Nagato* was a target ship for the US nuclear tests at Bikini; severely damaged in the second test, her wreck sank on 29 July.

SPECIFICATIONS

COUNTRY OF ORIGIN: Japan
CREW: 1333
WEIGHT: 39,116 tonnes (38,500 tons)
DIMENSIONS: 215.8m x 29m x 9m (708ft x 95ft 1in x 29ft 10in)
RANGE: 9900km (5500nm) at 10 knots
ARMOUR: 304–102mm (12–4in) belt, 304mm (12in) on barbettes and turrets
ARMAMENT: 8 x 406mm (16in), 20 x 140mm (5.5in) guns
POWERPLANT: quadruple-screw turbines
PERFORMANCE: 23 knots

Napoli

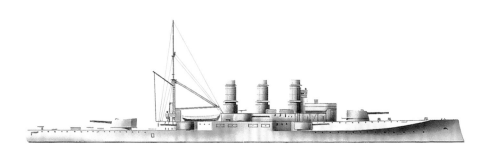

Napoli was designed by Vittorio Cuniberti, and evolved from a project to build an 8128-tonne (8000-ton) ship, protected with 152mm (6in) armour, armed with 12 x 203mm (8in) guns that could achieve 22 knots. From this idea, Cuniberti developed *Napoli*, a battleship that was faster than any afloat, as well as being far more powerful than any cruiser. Completed in 1907 as one of the Regina Elena class, she was a forerunner of the battlecruiser. Her 304mm (12in) guns were in turrets fore and aft, and the 203mm (8in) guns were in twin turrets, three on each beam. In 1911, *Napoli* took part in naval operations at Tobruk, and in the bombardment of Benghazi; in 1912, she saw action in the Dardanelles and the Aegean Sea, being part of the covering force during the Italian occupation of Rhodes. In World War I, she saw active service in the Adriatic. *Napoli* was removed from service in 1926.

SPECIFICATIONS

COUNTRY OF ORIGIN: Italy
CREW: 764
WEIGHT: 14,338 tonnes (14,112 tons)
DIMENSIONS: 144.6m x 22.4m x 8.5m (474ft 5in x 73ft 6in x 27ft 10in)
RANGE: 18,000km (10,000nm) at 12 knots
ARMOUR: 245mm (9.8in) on sides, 203mm (8in) on turrets
ARMAMENT: 2 x 304mm (12in), 12 x 203mm (8in) guns
POWERPLANT: twin-screw, vertical triple expansion engines
PERFORMANCE: 22 knots

Nassau

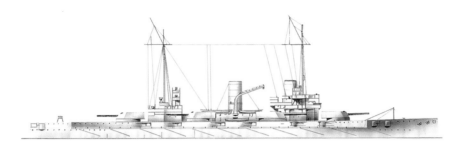

Nassau was laid down in 1906 as Germany's first dreadnought, though she was not commissioned until 1910. She was the first ship in the Nassau class, which also included *Westfalen*, *Posen* and *Rheinland*. Originally designed to carry only eight guns in her main armament, two extra double turrets were included in her construction which affected her performance, though she was still a steady gun platform. Present at the Battle of Jutland – during which she survived a collision with the British destroyer Spitfire – *Nassau* surrendered at the end of World War I and was scrapped in 1921. Of the other ships in her class, *Westfalen* survived being torpedoed by the British submarine E23 in August 1916 and was broken up in 1924; *Posen* collided with the cruiser *Elbing* at Jutland and was stricken in 1919; *Rheinland* went aground during landings in Finland in April 1918, and was stricken in 1919.

SPECIFICATIONS

COUNTRY OF ORIGIN: Germany
CREW: 966
WEIGHT: 20,533 tonnes (20,210 tons)
DIMENSIONS: 146m x 27m x 8.5m (479ft 4in x 88ft 3in x 27ft 10in)
RANGE: 10,556km (5700nm) at 10 knots
ARMOUR: 293–102mm (11.75–4in) belt, 304mm (12in) on turrets
ARMAMENT: 12 x 150mm (5.9in), 12 x 279mm (11in) guns
POWERPLANT: triple-screw, vertical triple expansion engines
PERFORMANCE: 20 knots

Nelson

Nelson and her sister ship, *Rodney*, were the first battleships to be completed within the limits of the Washington Treaty of 1922, which fixed the maximum displacement for each class of vessel. They were also the first British warships to carry 406mm (16in) guns. Completed in 1927, *Nelson*'s main armament was concentrated forward of the tower bridge in three triple turrets, saving on armour weight. More weight was saved by adopting less powerful machinery. The secondary battery was carried in twin turrets level with the main mast. The engine rooms were placed forward of the boiler rooms to keep the bridge structure clear of funnel smoke. *Nelson* was out of action for nearly a year after being torpedoed by Italian aircraft while escorting the Malta convoy 'Halberd' on 27 September 1941, and was damaged by a German torpedo off Normandy in July 1944. Both ships were scrapped in 1948–49.

SPECIFICATIONS

COUNTRY OF ORIGIN: United Kingdom
CREW: 1361 (as flagship)
WEIGHT: 38,608 tonnes (38,000 tons)
DIMENSIONS: 216.8m x 32.4m x 9.6m (711ft 3in x 106ft 4in x 31ft 6in)
RANGE: 30,574km (16,500nm) at 12 knots
ARMOUR: 356–330mm (14–13in) belt, 380–350mm (15–12in) on barbettes, 406mm (16in) on turrets
ARMAMENT: 9 x 406mm (16in), 12 x 152mm (6in) guns
POWERPLANT: twin-screw turbines
PERFORMANCE: 23.5 knots

Nevada

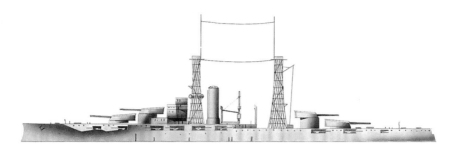

Nevada was one of the first battleships to be built on the 'all-or-nothing' principle, adopted by other navies after World War I, in which the thickest possible armour was applied to vital areas, leaving the rest virtually unprotected. She and her sister, *Oklahoma*, were second-generation dreadnoughts, and were the first US battleships to burn only oil fuel. Launched in 1914, and seeing service off Ireland in World War I, *Nevada* was badly damaged at Pearl Harbor in December 1941. After repairs, she served as one of the bombardment force of warships at the Normandy landings of June 1944, and off southern France in August before returning to the Pacific, where she was damaged by a kamikaze and shore batteries. In July 1946, *Nevada* was a target vessel at Bikini, an experience she survived. She was sunk as a target by aircraft and gunfire off Hawaii in July 1948.

SPECIFICATIONS

COUNTRY OF ORIGIN: United States
CREW: 1374 (during World War II)
WEIGHT: 29,362 tonnes (28,900 tons)
DIMENSIONS: 177.7m x 29m x 9.5m (583ft x 95ft 3in x 31ft 2in)
RANGE: 18,530km (10,000nm) at 10 knots
ARMOUR: 343–203mm (13.5–8in) belt, 450–229mm (18–9in) on turrets
ARMAMENT: 21 x 127mm (5in), 10 x 355mm (14in) guns
POWERPLANT: twin-screw turbines
PERFORMANCE: 20.5 knots

New York

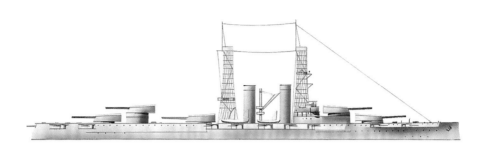

New York was laid down in September 1911 and completed in April 1914. Her engines developed 22,138kW (29,687hp) and coal supply was 2964 tonnes (2917 tons), plus 406 tonnes (400 tons) of fuel oil. In 1916, New York was the first American battleship to fit anti-aircraft guns. From 1914–19, she served with the US Atlantic Fleet, and for the last year of World War I she was assigned to the Royal Navy's Grand Fleet. After reconstruction work at Norfolk, during which her cage masts were replaced by tripods, New York was again assigned to the Atlantic Fleet from 1936 to 1941 and, in 1939, she was experimentally fitted with the first shipborne radar. Service in World War II took her to North Africa, Iwo Jima and Okinawa, where she was slightly damaged by a kamikaze. Having survived World War II, New York went on to survive the Bikini atomic bomb tests in 1946. She was sunk as a target off Pearl Harbor in 1948.

SPECIFICATIONS

COUNTRY OF ORIGIN: United States
CREW: 1042
WEIGHT: 28,854 tonnes (28,400 tons)
DIMENSIONS: 174.6m x 29m x 9m (572ft 10in x 95ft 2in x 29ft 6in)
RANGE: 12,708km (7060nm) at 12 knots
ARMOUR: 304–254mm (12–10in) belt and barbettes, 356mm (14in) on turrets
ARMAMENT: 10 x 356mm (14in), 21 x 127mm (5in) guns
POWERPLANT: twin-screw, triple expansion engines
PERFORMANCE: 21.4 knots

North Carolina

North Carolina and her sister, Washington, were the first US battleships built after the lifting of the 1922 Washington Naval Treaty. However, the original design followed the later London Treaty which allowed for 355mm (14in) guns, but, as the Japanese refused to restrict their main armament, the US decided to fit North Carolina with triple 400mm (16in) gun turrets after her launch in 1940. By 1945, her weaponry had been replaced by mainly anti-aircraft weapons, namely 96 x 40mm (1.6in), and 36 x 20mm (0.8in) guns. She fought in the Pacific, from Guadalcanal to the final strikes on Japan. On 15 September 1942, North Carolina was torpedoed by the Japanese submarine I-19 near Espiritu Santu, together with the destroyer USS O'Brien, which was sunk and, on 6 April 1945, she was hit by friendly fire off Okinawa. She was stricken in 1960, and is now preserved at Wilmington, North Carolina.

SPECIFICATIONS

COUNTRY OF ORIGIN: United States
CREW: 1880
WEIGHT: 47,518 tonnes (46,770 tons)
DIMENSIONS: 222m x 33m x 10m (728ft 9in x 108ft 3in x 32ft 10in)
RANGE: 32,334km (17,450nm) at 12 knots
ARMOUR: 304–165mm (12–6.6in) belt, 140mm (5.5in) on deck, 400mm (16in) on barbettes and turrets
ARMAMENT: 9 x 400mm (16in), 20 x 127mm (5in) guns
POWERPLANT: quadruple-screw turbines
PERFORMANCE: 28 knots

Pennsylvania

Pennsylvania was completed in 1916 and, with her sister, *Arizona*, boasted a main armament of 12 x 356mm (14in) guns triple-mounted in four turrets. The triple mount later became a characteristic of American capital ships. *Pennsylvania* was reconstructed between the wars to include a large anti-aircraft armament, two aircraft catapults, two tripod masts and a strengthened submarine bulge and bulkheads. She came through World War II, though *Arizona* did not, being destroyed at Pearl Harbor in 1941. *Pennsylvania* herself was damaged by bombs while in dry dock at Pearl Harbor and, after reconstruction, she fought at Attu, the Gilbert Islands, Kwajalein, Eniwetok, Saipan, Guam, Palau, Leyte Gulf, Surigao Strait and Lingayen. On 12 August 1945, she was severely damaged by an aerial torpedo. After the war *Pennsylvania* took part in two nuclear bomb tests, ending her days as a target ship.

SPECIFICATIONS

COUNTRY OF ORIGIN: United States
CREW: 915
WEIGHT: 33,088 tonnes (32,567 tons)
DIMENSIONS: 182.9m x 185.4 x 29.6m x 8.8m (600ft 1in x 97ft 1in x 28ft 10in)
RANGE: 14,400km (8000nm) at 12 knots
ARMOUR: 343–203mm (13.5–8in) belt, 450mm (18in) on turret
ARMAMENT: 12 x 356mm (14in), 22 x 127mm (5in) guns
POWERPLANT: four-shaft, geared turbines
PERFORMANCE: 21 knots

Pobieda

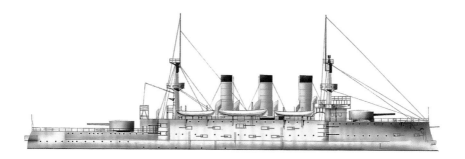

Completed in 1902, *Pobieda*'s engines developed 11,185kW (15,000hp), and coal supply was 2032 tonnes (2000 tons). *Pobieda*, *Peresviet* and *Osliabia* – all of the same class – were the first Russian warships to feature quick-firing guns. They had a high forecastle with their secondary armament mounted on two decks. *Pobieda* joined the Pacific squadron in 1903, in time for the war with Japan. In February 1904, she was slightly damaged by gunfire in action at Port Arthur, and further damaged by a mine in April, but survived thanks to the protection given by her coal bunker and internal armour. On 10 August, *Pobieda* took 11 hits in the Battle of the Yellow Sea, and was again repeatedly hit by shore batteries in October–November. In December 1904, she was sunk by salvos of 279mm (11in) shells, but raised by the Japanese in 1905 and renamed *Suwo*. She was scrapped in 1922.

SPECIFICATIONS

COUNTRY OF ORIGIN: Russia
CREW: 757
WEIGHT: 12,872 tonnes (12,670 tons)
DIMENSIONS: 133m x 21.7m x 8.3m (436ft 4in x 71ft 5in x 27ft 3in)
RANGE: 11,118km (6000nm) at 10 knots
ARMOUR: 229–127mm (9–5in) belt, 254–127mm (10–5in) on turrets, 127mm (5in) on casemates
ARMAMENT: 4 x 254mm (10in), 11 x 152mm (6in), 20 x 75mm (3in), guns
POWERPLANT: triple-screw, vertical triple expansion engines
PERFORMANCE: 18.5 knots

Prince of Wales

Prince of Wales was launched in 1939 and completed in 1941. Her main armament was housed in two quadruple 356mm (14in) gun turrets fore and aft and a double 356mm (14in) turret superfiring forward. She took part in the hunt for the *Bismarck* in May 1941 with her construction incomplete and workers still on her. While engaging the German battleship she took hits on her bridge and below her waterline but survived. In August 1941, she took Winston Churchill to an historic meeting with President Franklin D. Roosevelt in Newfoundland. Later in 1941, she was sent to the Far East as a last-minute defence against the Japanese invasion of Malaya. With the battlecruiser *Repulse* and four destroyers, she sortied on 9 December. The next day, she and *Repulse* were attacked by Japanese aircraft and within two hours both had been sunk. *Prince of Wales* had been operational for less than a year.

SPECIFICATIONS

COUNTRY OF ORIGIN: United Kingdom
CREW: 1422
WEIGHT: 41,402 tonnes (42,076 tons)
DIMENSIONS: 227.1m x 31.4m x 9.9m (745ft 1in x 103ft x 32ft 7in)
RANGE: 25,942km (14,000nm) at 10 knots
ARMOUR: 380–112mm (15–4.5in) belt, 330–279mm (13–11in) on barbettes, 330–152mm (13–6in) on turrets
ARMAMENT: 10 x 356mm (14in), 16 x 131mm (5.25in) guns
POWERPLANT: four-shaft, geared turbines
PERFORMANCE: 28 knots

Príncipe de Asturias

The Spanish carrier *Príncipe de Asturias* was laid down in 1979, but commissioning was delayed until 1988 to allow an advanced digital command and control system to be fitted. The vessel is based on the US Sea Control Ship concept and can accomodate up to 29 aircraft if necessary. More commonly, twelve Harrier Short Takeoff/Vertical Landing aircraft are carried. These are launched with the assistance of a 'ski jump' ramp at the fore end of the flight deck. *Príncipe de Asturias* also normally carries a mix of 12 helicopters. Like most carriers, *Príncipe de Asturias* relies on its air group for offensive capability and is armed only for self-defence with four 20mm (0.79in) Close-In Weapon Systems for missile and air defence, backed up by decoy launchers and electronic countermeasures. A mid-life upgrade is planned, which will improve the vessel's performance in the littoral environment where modern naval operations increasingly take place.

SPECIFICATIONS

COUNTRY OF ORIGIN: Spain
CREW: 763 (total); 600 ship crew, 230 air crew
WEIGHT: 15,912 tonnes (15,661 tons) standard, 16,700 (16,436) tons loaded
DIMENSIONS: 195.9m x 24.3m x 9.4m (643ft x 80ft x 31ft)
RANGE: 12,000km (6500nm) at 20 knots
ARMOUR: unknown
ARMAMENT: 4 x ABA Meroka mod 2B 20mm (0.79in) guns
POWERPLANT: 2 x General Electric LM2500+ gas turbines in COGAG configuration, 1 x shaft, 34,600kW (46,400hp)
PERFORMANCE: 26 knots

Queen Elizabeth

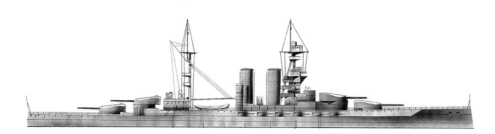

Completed in 1915, *Queen Elizabeth* was a major advance in battleship development, and was the first capital ship to be built with oil-burning boilers. She was fast, but her reliance upon oil fuel concerned critics, who foresaw disaster if oil supplies were ever interrupted. As a result, the following Revenge class carried both coal and oil fuel. She saw service in the Dardanelles in 1915, but missed the Battle of Jutland the following year due to a refit. Converted to a flagship, *Queen Elizabeth* was rebuilt between 1937–41. Assigned to the Mediterranean Fleet, she was in action off Crete in May 1941. In December that year, she was severely damaged in a daring attack by Italian frogmen in Alexandria harbour. In 1943–44 she served with the Home Fleet, then sailed for the Indian Ocean, where she completed her war service. She was scrapped in 1948–49.

SPECIFICATIONS

COUNTRY OF ORIGIN: United Kingdom
CREW: 951
WEIGHT: 33,548 tonnes (33,020 tons)
DIMENSIONS: 196.8m x 27.6m x 10m (645ft 8in x 90ft 6in x 32ft 10in)
RANGE: 8100km (4500nm) at 10 knots
ARMOUR: 330–152mm (13–6in) belt, 254–102mm (10–4in) on barbettes, 330mm (13in) on turrets
ARMAMENT: 8 x 380mm (15in), 16 x 152mm (6in) guns
POWERPLANT: quadruple-screw turbines
PERFORMANCE: 23 knots

Queen Elizabeth (CVF)

Construction began in 2009 on a pair of large conventionally powered carriers for the Royal Navy. HMS *Queen Elizabeth* is expected to enter service in 2016, with her sister *Prince of Wales* following in 2018. These vessels are to replace the existing Invincible class, and are vastly more capable. Displacing three times as much as the Invincibles, the Queen Elizabeth class is designed to operate an air group of 40 aircraft including the F-35 Joint Strike Fighter and Merlin helicopters. However, the vessels' planned 50-year service life is expected to far exceed that of the selected air assets. The design incorporates the capability of upgrade to accommodate future aircraft. This may necessitate the removal of the 'ski jump' ramp at the front of the launch deck and its replacement with a catapult system. Defensive armament systems may also be added if budget funds become available. These will likely take the form of vertically launched Aster missiles.

SPECIFICATIONS

COUNTRY OF ORIGIN: United Kingdom
CREW: 600 (1450 capacity)
WEIGHT: 65,600 tonnes (64,564 tons) (full)
DIMENSIONS: 284m x 39m x 11m (931ft 9in x 128ft x 36ft 1in)
RANGE: 10,000 nautical miles (18,520km)
ARMOUR: unknown
ARMAMENT: 40 aircraft, including 36 F-35 Lightning II
POWERPLANT: 2 x Rolls-Royce Marine 36MW (48hp) MT30 gas turbine alternators, providing over 70MW (93.8hp); plus 4 x diesel engines providing 40MW (53.6hp)
PERFORMANCE: 25+ knots

Regina Margherita

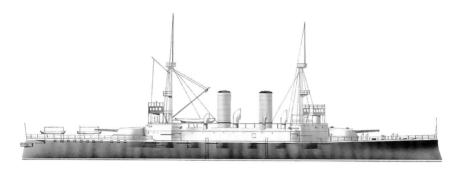

Regina Margherita was designed by Benedetto Brin, with the emphasis placed on speed. As originally designed, the vessel was to have had 4 x 304mm (12in) guns, together with 12 x 203mm (8in) weapons. However, after Brin's death, the plans were revised to feature the mixed armament listed in the specifications. An unusual feature of her design was the double bridge fore and aft. Regina Margherita sank in 1916 after striking two German mines laid off Valona by the German submarine UC14. The loss of life (675) was heavy. They were casualties in a theatre of war often eclipsed by the carnage of the Western Front, but it was of vital importance to the eventual Allied victory. If the Central Powers had succeeded in securing Albania as one of their principalities and had fortified Valona, they could have closed the Adriatic. The Italians prevented them from doing so.

SPECIFICATIONS

COUNTRY OF ORIGIN: Italy
CREW: 900
WEIGHT: 13,426 tonnes (13,215 tons)
DIMENSIONS: 138.6m x 23.8m x 8.8m (454ft 10in x 78ft 3in x 28ft 10in)
RANGE: 18,000km (10,000nm) at 12 knots
ARMOUR: 152mm (6in) on side, 203mm (8in) on turrets, 152mm (6in) on battery
ARMAMENT: 4 x 304mm (12in), 12 x 152mm (6in), 20 x 75mm (3in) guns
POWERPLANT: twin-screw, triple expansion engines
PERFORMANCE: 20.3 knots

Renown

Constructed in just a year, *Renown* and her sister, *Repulse*, were the last British battlecruisers. Heavily armed, but sacrificing protective armour for high speed; within a month of her launch in October 1916, *Renown* was back in dock to be fitted with another 492 tonnes (500 tons) of steel plate. Even then she was thought to be too lightly built, even for the recoil of her 380mm (15in) guns, and was to receive extra armour during refits in 1918 and 1923. Converted into a fast carrier escort in 1936, *Renown* took part in operations against commerce raiders in the South Atlantic in 1939 and was damaged in action off Norway in April 1940. She subsequently took part in the hunt for *Bismarck*, escorted convoys to Malta, in the Atlantic and the Arctic, and formed part of the covering force during the Allied landings in North Africa. She served with the Eastern Fleet in 1944–45 and was broken up at Faslane in 1948.

SPECIFICATIONS

COUNTRY OF ORIGIN: United Kingdom
CREW: 1200
WEIGHT: 30,356 tonnes (30,850 tons)
DIMENSIONS: 242.2m x 27.4m x 7.8m (794ft 7in x 90ft x 25ft 6in)
RANGE: 6570km (3650nm) at 12 knots
ARMOUR: 152–37.5mm (6–1.5in) belt, 178–102mm (7–4in) on barbettes, 279mm (11in) on turrets
ARMAMENT: 6 x 380mm (15in), 17 x 102mm (4in) guns
POWERPLANT: four-shaft, geared turbines
PERFORMANCE: 30 knots

Retvisan

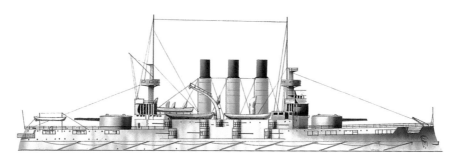

Retvisan was the only capital ship to be built for the Russians by a US yard, and her design was standard US type, with a flush-deck and central superstructure. During the Russo-Japanese war in 1904, she was torpedoed off Port Arthur. She survived, but was later hit by howitzers during the Battle of the Yellow Sea and sunk. When Port Arthur fell in 1905, she was raised by the Japanese. Renamed *Hizen*, she was used as a target and finally sunk in 1924. Numerically, the Russian Far Eastern and Japanese fleets were not dissimilar, but Japan commanded the approaches to Port Arthur and Vladivostok. The former was attacked without declaration of war by Japanese destroyers on the night of 8/9 February 1904, two battleships (one the *Retvisan*) and a cruiser being damaged. Weeks later a Japanese invasion force laid siege to the base, precipitating the war that resulted in the destruction of the Russian fleet at Tsushima.

SPECIFICATIONS

COUNTRY OF ORIGIN: Russia
CREW: 738
WEIGHT: 13,106 tonnes (12,900 tons)
DIMENSIONS: 117.8m x 22m x 7.9m (386ft 8in x 72ft 2in x 26ft)
RANGE: 7412km (4000nm) at 10 knots
ARMOUR: 229–127mm (9–5in) belt, 229–203mm (9–8in) on turrets
ARMAMENT: 4 x 304mm (12in), 12 x 152mm (6in), 20 x 11-pounder guns
POWERPLANT: twin-screw, vertical triple expansion engines
PERFORMANCE: 18.8 knots

Richelieu

Richelieu was first in a class of four battleships planned between 1935 and 1938, but she was the only one completed in time to see action during World War II. Launched in March 1940, *Richelieu* escaped the fall of France and joined the Allies in 1942, forming part of a powerful battle group that included battleships *Valiant*, *Howe* and *Queen Elizabeth*, battlecruiser *Renown* and carriers *Victorious*, *Illustrious* and *Indomitable*. She escorted many attack sorties by the carriers on Java, Sumatra and the various enemy-held island groups in the Indian Ocean. *Richelieu* underwent a substantial refit in the USA in 1943, when radar and an extra 100 antiaircraft guns were added. Joining the British Eastern Fleet in 1944, she served until the end of the war. She later operated off Indo-China during France's war there. *Richelieu* was paid off and hulked in 1959, and was broken up in 1964.

SPECIFICATIONS

COUNTRY OF ORIGIN: France
CREW: 1670
WEIGHT: 47,000 tonnes (47,8500 tons)
DIMENSIONS: 247.85m x 33m x 9.63m (813ft 2in x 108ft 3in x 32ft 8in)
RANGE: 10,800km (6000nm) at 12 knots
ARMOUR: 342–243mm (13.5–9.75in) belt
ARMAMENT: 8 x 380mm (15in), 9 x 152mm (6in) guns
POWERPLANT: 4 x Parsons geared turbines; 6 x Indret Sural boilers
PERFORMANCE: 30 knots

Ryujo

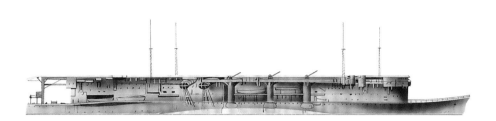

L aunched in 1931, *Ryujo* was Japan's first major purpose-built aircraft carrier. She was designed with a cruiser hull, which restricted her width, so a second hangar was built above the first. This resulted in increased top weight and instability and, almost immediately after her completion in May 1933, she was back in the dockyards for modification. Between 1934 and 1936 her hull was strengthened and her bulges widened. In December 1941, *Ryujo* was one of the ships covering the Japanese landings in the Philippines, followed by the Dutch East Indies in February 1942. The following April, she formed part of the Japanese carrier task force that made a major sortie into the Indian Ocean to strike at Ceylon. She subsequently moved back to the Pacific for operations against Midway Island, and was sunk by aircraft from USS *Saratoga* in August 1942 during the battle of the Eastern Solomons.

SPECIFICATIONS

COUNTRY OF ORIGIN: Japan
CREW: 924 (after 1936)
WEIGHT: 10,150 tonnes (9990 tons)
DIMENSIONS: 175.3m x 23m x 5.5m (575ft 5in x 75ft 6in x 18ft 3in)
RANGE: 18,530km (10,000nm) at 14 knots
ARMOUR: light plate around magazines and machinery
ARMAMENT: 12 x 127mm (5in) guns
POWERPLANT: twin-screw, turbines
PERFORMANCE: 29 knots

Scharnhorst

Launched in 1936, *Scharnhorst* and her sister, *Gneisenau*, were designed as fast commerce raiders. Though outgunned by the 400mm (16in) weapons of British battleships, plans existed to improve the main armament to 380mm (15in). War intervened and proposed turrets for bigger guns went to the *Bismarck*. *Scharnhorst* took part in the invasion of Norway in April 1940 where she was damaged. Despite this, she sank the carrier *Glorious* the following month. Considered a deadly threat, she was attacked for the next two years by surface ships, aircraft and minisubmarines, but remained operational. In February 1942, *Scharnhorst* escaped from the French port of Brest, to make a famous dash through the English Channel. She was mined and damaged en route. *Scharnhorst* was finally sunk in December 1943 by Duke of York and three cruisers on her way to attack an Arctic convoy.

SPECIFICATIONS

COUNTRY OF ORIGIN: Germany
CREW: 1840
WEIGHT: 38,277 tonnes (38,900 tons)
DIMENSIONS: 229.8m x 30m x 9.91m (753ft 11in x 98ft 5in x 32ft 6in)
RANGE: 16,306km (8800nm) at 19 knots
ARMOUR: 343–168mm (13.75–6.75in) belt, 356–152mm (14–6in) on main turrets, 75mm (3in) on deck
ARMAMENT: 9 x 279mm (11in), 12 x 150mm (5.8in) guns
POWERPLANT: three-shaft, geared turbines
PERFORMANCE: 32 knots

Shinano

At the time of her completion, *Shinano* was the world's largest aircraft carrier, but she was to have the shortest career of any major warship of her type when, on 29 November 1944, she was sunk by the US submarine *Archerfish*. *Shinano* was a Yamato class battleship, but, after carrier losses at the Battle of Midway, she was converted into an auxiliary carrier with massive internal capacity for transporting supplies of fuel and spares, plus aircraft, to the Japanese task forces. Her single-storey hangar was 168m (550ft) long, and her own air group of 40–50 planes were housed forward, with the replacement aircraft for the task forces stowed aft. *Shinano* was torpedoed and sunk while on her way to Kure for final fitting out. There is little doubt that the decisive Battle of Midway turned the tide of the Pacific war. The lack of strong carrier forces afterwards put an end to Japanese hopes of further conquest.

SPECIFICATIONS

COUNTRY OF ORIGIN: Japan
CREW: 2400
WEIGHT: 74,208 tonnes 973,040 tons)
DIMENSIONS: 266m x 40m x 10.3m (872ft 9in x 131ft 3in x 33ft 9in)
RANGE: 13,340km (7200nm) at 16 knots
ARMOUR: 202mm (8.1in) belt, 77.5mm (3.1in) on flight deck, 187mm (7.5in) on hangar deck
ARMAMENT: 16 x 127mm (5in), 145 x 25mm (1in) guns, 336 x rocket launchers, 70 x aircraft
POWERPLANT: quadruple-screw turbines
PERFORMANCE: 28 knots

South Dakota

Commissioned into service in 1942, *South Dakota* was the first in a class of four battleships designed specifically to survive hits from 400mm (16in) shells while being able to perform at up to 27 knots. Launched in June 1941, *South Dakota* was fitted as a purposely designed force flagship. She saw service off Guadalcanal in 1942, where she was instrumental in defending the Enterprise task group, and later took part in the night action which saw the destruction of the Japanese battleship *Kirishima*. In 1944, *South Dakota* was in action during the Battle of the Philippine Sea, and was present at Tokyo Bay at the formal Japanese surrender in August 1945, when she flew the flag of the commander of the US Pacific Fleet, Adm Halsey. She was damaged in action three times: at the Battle of Santa Cruz, at Guadalcanal, and off Saipan. *South Dakota* was withdrawn from service in 1946 and sold in 1962.

SPECIFICATIONS

COUNTRY OF ORIGIN: United Kingdom
CREW: 1793
WEIGHT: 43,806 tonnes (44,519 tons)
DIMENSIONS: 207.3m x 34m x 10.7m (680ft 1in x 108ft 2in x 35ft 1in)
RANGE: 27,000km (15,000nm) at 12 knots
ARMOUR: 304mm (12in) belt, 282–432mm (11.3–17.3in) on barbettes, 450mm (18in) on turrets
ARMAMENT: 9 x 400mm (16in), 20 x 127mm (5in) guns
POWERPLANT: four-shaft turbines
PERFORMANCE: 27.5 knots

Taiho

Taiho (Giant Phoenix) was Japan's largest purpose-built aircraft carrier and the first to feature an armoured deck. She was laid down in July 1941 and went into service in March 1944. The two-tier hangars were 150m (500ft) long and unarmoured at the sides. The lower hangar was 124mm (4.9in) thick over the boiler and machinery spaces, which also had 150mm- (5.9in-) thick side armour, and the flight deck had 75mm- (3in-) thick armour to withstand a 455kg (1000lb) bomb. Total armour protection came to 8940 tonnes (8800 tons). Taiho was blown up within a few weeks of entering service by the US submarine Albacore on 19 June 1944, during the Battle of the Philippine Sea. Two more vessels of this class were planned (Nos 801 and 802) together with five more of a modified Taiho type (Nos 5021 to 5025) but none was ever laid down. Taiho was similar in design to the earlier Shokaku.

SPECIFICATIONS

COUNTRY OF ORIGIN: Japan
CREW: 1751
WEIGHT: 37,866 tonnes (37,270 tons)
DIMENSIONS: 260.6m x 30m x 9.6m (855ft x 98ft 6in x 31ft 6in)
RANGE: 14,824km (8000nm) at 18 knots
ARMOUR: 150–55mm (5.5–2.2in) belt, 77.5mm (3.1in) on flight deck
ARMAMENT: 12 x 100mm (3.9in), 71 x 25mm (1in) guns
POWERPLANT: quadruple-screw turbines
PERFORMANCE: 33.3 knots

Tiger

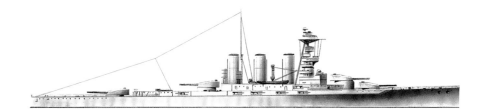

Completed in 1914, it had been intended to fit *Tiger* with small tube boilers and geared turbines and, had this suggestion been adopted, her top speed may have been 32 knots. However, as it was, *Tiger* was still the fastest – as well as the largest – capital ship of her day. She was also the last coal-burning capital ship in the Royal Navy, and was the only British battlecruiser to carry 152mm (6in) guns. She took part in the battles of Dogger Bank in 1915 and Jutland in 1916, receiving 15 direct hits during the latter. Battlecruisers such as *Tiger* were vulnerable when unable to exploit their speed and firepower, but survival depended on where they were hit, not the number of times. *Tiger* took 15 hits and survived, but the three battlecruisers that were sunk were struck by just six 279mm (11in) and 305mm (12in) shells. After World War I, *Tiger* served in the Atlantic Fleet until becoming a training ship in 1924. She was paid off in 1933.

SPECIFICATIONS

COUNTRY OF ORIGIN: United Kingdom
CREW: 1121
WEIGHT: 35,723 tonnes (35,160 tons)
DIMENSIONS: 214.6m x 27.6m x 8.6m (704ft 1in x 90ft 6in x 28ft 5in)
RANGE: 8370km (4650nm) at 12 knots
ARMOUR: 229–75mm (9–3in) belt, 229mm (9in) on turrets and barbettes
ARMAMENT: 8 x 343mm (13.5in), 12 x 152mm (6in) guns
POWERPLANT: quadruple-screw turbines
PERFORMANCE: 30 knots

Tromp

Tromp and her sister ship, *Jacob van Heemskerck*, were interesting in being more 'pocket cruisers' than destroyers. They demonstrated how – at the top of the size scale – the distinction between the two could be blurred. The pair had true destroyer ancestry, however, being classed as leaders. Their design was enlarged, and welding and aluminium were extensively used in order to save weight. An interesting reflection on *Tromp*'s use in the vast Dutch East Indies was the incorporation of a Fokker seaplane. *Tromp* was completed in August 1938 and deployed to the Far East at the outbreak of war, being extensively damaged during the Japanese invasion of Bali. She survived the war, and took part in the reoccupation of the East Indies in September 1945. The Heemskerck served alongside British naval forces in the Indian Ocean and Mediterranean.

SPECIFICATIONS

COUNTRY OF ORIGIN: Netherlands
CREW: not known
WEIGHT: 4979 tonnes (4900 tons)
DIMENSIONS: 131.9m x 12.41m x 5.41m (432ft 9in x 40ft 9in x 17ft 9in)
RANGE: not known
ARMOUR: not known
ARMAMENT: four 304mm (12in), 12 152mm (6in), 20 3-pounder guns
POWERPLANT: twin-shafts, two sets of geared steam turbines
PERFORMANCE: 32.5 knots

Tsessarevitch

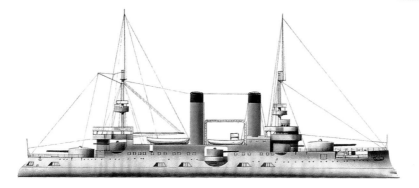

Tsessarevitch was part of the Russian naval expansion programme of 1898. She was laid down at La Seyne in June 1899, and was completed in 1903. Her design followed the French practice of the period, having a pronounced tumble-home and high forecastle. Assigned to the Pacific Fleet, where she flew the flag of Rear Adm Vitgeft, commanding the First Pacific Squadron, Tsessarevitch was damaged in the surprise Japanese attack on Port Arthur on 9 February 1904. On 7 August that year, she was hit by siege batteries at Port Arthur and, three days later, she was damaged by 15 hits in the Battle of the Yellow Sea, Rear Adm Vitgeft being killed in the action. She was later interned at Kiauchau, China. While serving in the Baltic in World War I, during which time she engaged the German dreadnought Kronprinz, she was renamed Grazhdanin. She was scrapped in 1922.

SPECIFICATIONS

COUNTRY OF ORIGIN: Russia
CREW: 782
WEIGHT: 13,122 tonnes (12,915 tons)
DIMENSIONS: 118.5m x 23.2m x 7.9m (388ft 9in x 76ft 1in x 26ft)
RANGE: 10,192km (5500nm) at 10 knots
ARMOUR: 254–178mm (10–7in) belt, 254mm (10in) on main turrets, 152mm (6in) on secondary turrets
ARMAMENT: four 304mm (12in), 12 152mm (6in), 20 3-pounder guns
POWERPLANT: twin-screw, vertical triple expansion engines
PERFORMANCE: 18.5 knots

Tsukuba

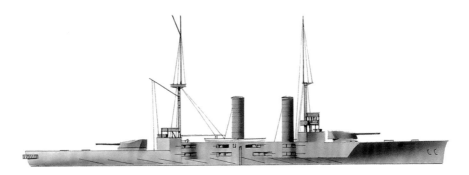

Tsukuba was ordered in 1904 as a replacement for one of two powerful battleships lost during the war with Russia. She was laid down at Kure Naval Dockyard in 1905, and originally classified as an armoured cruiser. By the time she was completed in 1907, much more powerful battlecruisers were being built for the Japanese Navy, and in 1921 her sister, *Ikoma*, was rerated as a first-class cruiser. In January 1917, *Tsukuba*'s magazine caught fire and she blew up in Yokosuka Bay killing 305 crew. She was later raised and broken up. In 1914, as part of the Imperial Japanese Navy's 1st South Seas Squadron, *Tsukuba* took part in the search for the German Adm von Spee's battle squadron, which had been sighted east of the Marshall Islands. Adm von Spee eluded his pursuers and went on to win the Battle of Coronel in November 1914, but was defeated and killed off the Falklands on 8 December.

SPECIFICATIONS

COUNTRY OF ORIGIN: Japan
CREW: 879
WEIGHT: 15,646 tonnes (15,400 tons)
DIMENSIONS: 137m x 23m x 8m (449ft 10in x 75ft 6in x 26ft 3in)
RANGE: 7412km (4000nm) at 14 knots
ARMOUR: 178–102mm (7–4in) belt, 178mm (7in) on turrets and barbettes, 75mm (3in) on deck
ARMAMENT: 4 x 304mm (12in), 12 x 152mm (6in) guns
POWERPLANT: twin-screw, vertical triple expansion engines
PERFORMANCE: 20.5 knots

Unicorn

Launched in 1941, *Unicorn* was built as part of the 1938 Naval Expansion Programme, and was intended to be a depot/maintenance support ship. She was modified during construction so that she could operate her own aircraft, as well as maintain aircraft from other carriers. Her engines developed 29,828kW (40,000hp), and range at 13 knots was 20,900km (11,000 miles). After completion in 1943, she served in the Mediterranean, then on Atlantic patrols, before moving to the Pacific. She later became a depot ship in Hong Kong, and was scrapped in 1959–60. In Royal Navy circles, *Unicorn* is well remembered for her role in the Korean War, ferrying aircraft, spare parts and personnel to the theatre. The British Commonwealth air commitment in Korea comprised a squadron of Gloster Meteor fighters (RAAF) and 13 naval air squadrons on five light fleet carriers.

SPECIFICATIONS

COUNTRY OF ORIGIN: United Kingdom
CREW: 1200
WEIGHT: 20,624 tonnes (20,300 tons)
DIMENSIONS: 186m x 27.4m x 7.3m (610ft 3in x 90ft x 24ft)
RANGE: 20,900km (11,000nm) at 13 knots
ARMOUR: 12.5mm (4.5in) flight deck, 51mm (2in) belt
ARMAMENT: 8 x 102mm (4in) guns
POWERPLANT: twin-screw turbines
PERFORMANCE: 24 knots

V

Vanguard

Vanguard was the last battleship built for the Royal Navy. She was ordered in 1941 under the Emergency War Plan of 1940, but did not enter service until 1946. Vanguard was basically a lengthened King George V, and could accommodate four twin turrets on the centreline. In 1947, she took members of the British Royal Family on tour to South Africa and, after a refit, Vanguard served in the Mediterranean from 1949–51, primarily as a training ship. In the 1950s, she became part of the NATO reserve. The decision to complete the building of Vanguard was prompted both by the desire to have at least one modern capital ship embracing war experience (which in the event she did not have) and the availability of the twin 381mm (15in) guns removed from Courageous and Glorious when the latter ships were converted to aircraft carriers. She was sold for scrap in 1960.

SPECIFICATIONS

COUNTRY OF ORIGIN: United Kingdom
CREW: 1893
WEIGHT: 52,243 tonnes (51,420 tons)
DIMENSIONS: 248m x 32.9m x 10.9m (813ft 8in x 108ft x 35ft 9in)
RANGE: 16,677km (9000nm) at 20 knots
ARMOUR: 356–112mm (14–4.5in) belt, 330–152mm (13–6in) on main turrets, 330–280mm (13–11in) on barbettes
ARMAMENT: 8 x 380mm (15in), 16 x 140mm (5.5in) guns
POWERPLANT: quadruple-screw turbines
PERFORMANCE: 30 knots

Vittorio Emanuele

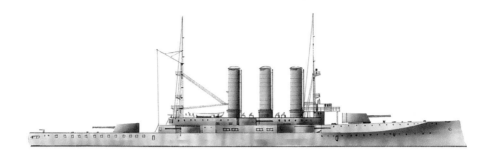

Vittorio Emanuele was one of a quartet of battleships of the Regina Elena class. They were built to a revolutionary design which combined a powerful armament with good protection and high speed on a relatively light displacement. The 304mm (12in) guns were mounted in single turrets, one forward and one aft, and the 203mm (8in) guns were in twin turrets at main deck level. Vittorio Emanuele was laid down in 1901 and completed in 1908. In 1911, she took part in naval operations off Tobruk and in the bombardment of Benghazi; the following year found her in the Aegean, providing support for Italian forces occupying the island of Rhodes. In 1915–17, she served in the southern Adriatic, returning to the Aegean in 1918. Her last active service was at Constantinople in 1919, during a period of civil unrest in Turkey. She was removed from service in 1923.

SPECIFICATIONS
COUNTRY OF ORIGIN: Italy
CREW: 764
WEIGHT: 12,800 tonnes (12,600 tons) (approx)
DIMENSIONS: 144.6m x 22.4m x 8m (474ft 4in x 73ft 6in x 26ft 3in)
RANGE: 18,000km (10,000nm) at 12 knots
ARMOUR: 245mm (9.8in) on sides, 37.5mm (1.5in) on deck, 203mm (8in) on turrets
ARMAMENT: 2 x 304mm (12in), 12 x 203mm (8in), 16 x 76mm (3in) guns
POWERPLANT: twin-screw, vertical triple expansion engines
PERFORMANCE: 21.3 knots

Vittorio Veneto

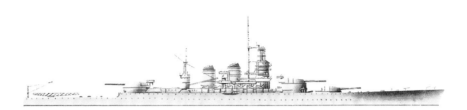

Vittorio Veneto was badly damaged several times during World War II. She was hit by a torpedo during the Battle of Matapan in March 1941. During this attack, which was carried out by Swordfish aircraft from the carrier HMS *Formidable*, *Veneto* narrowly escaped destruction. Out of three torpedoes dropped at close range to port and two to starboard, one struck her just above her port outer propeller, quickly flooding her with thousands of tons of water. *Veneto* managed to get away, but the Italians lost three cruisers, two destroyers and 2400 men. Having been repaired, she was torpedoed again, this time by the submarine *Urge*. As a finale she was bombed in 1943 on her way to Malta to surrender. After Italy joined the Allies, she was laid up in the Suez Canal. She was broken up between 1948 and 1950.

SPECIFICATIONS

COUNTRY OF ORIGIN: Italy
CREW: 1950
WEIGHT: 46,484 tonnes (45,752 tons)
DIMENSIONS: 237.8m x 32.9m x 9.6m (780ft 2in x 108ft x 31ft 6in)
RANGE: 8487km (4580nm) at 16 knots
ARMOUR: 279–75mm (11–3in) belt, 350–279mm (13.6–11in) on barbettes, 350–200mm (13.6–7.8in) on turrets
ARMAMENT: 9 x 381mm (15in), 12 x 152mm (6in), 4 x 120mm (4.7in), 12 x 89mm (3.5in) guns
POWERPLANT: quadruple-screw turbines
PERFORMANCE: 31.4 knots

Von der Tann

Completed in 1911, *Von der Tann* was Germany's first battlecruiser, and the first major German warship to have turbines. On 16 December 1914, following an earlier attack on Yarmouth, *Von der Tann* and other warships shelled Hartlepool, Whitby and Scarborough on the northeast coast of England, killing 127 civilians and wounding 567. The fact that 38 women and 39 children were among the dead caused a great anti-German outcry in Britain. *Von der Tann*'s protection was good and, though she was hit by four shells at the Battle of Jutland in 1916, which caused severe fire damage and put all her main guns out of action, she reached home without difficulty. She was surrendered at the end of World War I, and scuttled at Scapa Flow in June 1919. She was raised in December 1930, and was broken up at Rosyth between 1931 and 1934.

SPECIFICATIONS

COUNTRY OF ORIGIN: Germany
CREW: 1174 (at Jutland)
WEIGHT: 22,150 tonnes (21,802 tons)
DIMENSIONS: 172m x 26.6m x 8m (563ft 4in x 87ft 3in x 26ft 7in)
RANGE: 7920km (4400nm) at 10 knots
ARMOUR: 248–100mm (9.6–3.9in) belt, 228mm (8.8in) on barbettes and turrets
ARMAMENT: 8 x 280mm (11in), 10 x 150mm (5.9in) guns
POWERPLANT: quadruple-screw turbines
PERFORMANCE: 27.7 knots

Warspite

Completed in 1916, *Warspite* belonged to the Queen Elizabeth class, developed from the Iron Duke class, but her displacement was increased by 2540 tonnes (2500 tons), and 6m (20ft) were added to the length. The 380mm (15in) guns fired an 871kg (1916lb) shell to a range of 32km (20 miles) with extreme accuracy. She was badly damaged at Jutland, taking 15 hits from 279mm (11in) 304mm (12in) shells. *Warspite* was extensively modernized between 1934 and 1937. During operations in World War II, she was severely damaged by German bombs off Crete, and later by German radio-controlled bombs off Salerno, Italy, when covering the Allied landings. She was partially repaired, and used as part of the bombardment force covering the D-Day landings in Normandy. *Warspite* was further damaged by a mine off Harwich on 13 June 1944. She was paid off in 1945 and scrapped in 1948.

SPECIFICATIONS

COUNTRY OF ORIGIN: United Kingdom
CREW: 951
WEIGHT: 33,548 tonnes (33,020 tons)
DIMENSIONS: 197m x 28m x 9m (646ft 4in x 90ft 6in x 29ft 10in)
RANGE: 8100km (4500nm) at 10 knots
ARMOUR: 330–168mm (13–6.6in) belt, 330–127mm (13–5in) on turrets, 254–102mm (10–4in) on barbettes
ARMAMENT: 8 x 380mm (15in), 16 x 152mm (6in) guns
POWERPLANT: quadruple-screw turbines
PERFORMANCE: 23 knots

Washington

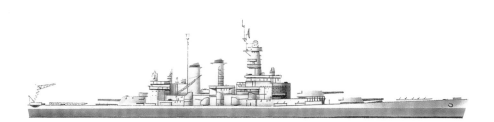

Washington and her sister, *North Carolina*, were the first US battleships built after the lifting of the 1922 Washington Naval Treaty. Original designs complied with the 356mm (14in) gun limitations of the later London Treaty, but, when Japan refused to ratify the agreement, the design was recast to carry three triple 400mm (16in) gun turrets. The additional weight of the larger weapons caused a two-knot reduction in top speed. *Washington* began her World War II service escorting Arctic convoys to Russia, then transferring to the Pacific Theatre, where she fought at Guadalcanal, Leyte, Okinawa and Iwo Jima and took part in many raids on Japanese-held territory. She suffered damage in a collision with the battleship *Indiana* in February 1944. *Washington*, along with *South Dakota*, sank the Japanese battlecruiser *Kirishima* at Guadalcanal in November 1942. She was scrapped in 1960–61.

SPECIFICATIONS

COUNTRY OF ORIGIN: United States
CREW: 1880
WEIGHT: 47,518 tonnes (46,770 tons)
DIMENSIONS: 222m x 33m x 10m (728ft 9in x 108ft 4in x 32ft 10in)
RANGE: 31,410km (17,450nm) at 12 knots
ARMOUR: 168–304mm belt (6.6–12in), 178–406mm (7–16in) on main turrets
ARMAMENT: 9 x 400mm (16in), 20 x 127mm (5in) guns
POWERPLANT: quadruple-screw turbines
PERFORMANCE: 28 knots

Yamato

Yamato, together with her sister *Musashi*, were the world's largest and most powerful battleships ever built when they were launched. No fewer than 23 designs were prepared for *Yamato* between 1934 and 1937 when she was laid down. When she was launched, her displacement was only surpassed by that of the British liner *Queen Mary*. Her main turrets each weighed 2818 tonnes (2774 tons), and each 460mm (18.1in) gun could fire two 1473kg (3240lb) shells per minute over a distance of 41km (25 miles). As flagship of the Combined Fleet, *Yamato* saw action in the battles of Midway, the Philippine Sea and Leyte Gulf. On 25 December 1943, she was torpedoed by the US submarine *Skate* south of Truk, and in October 1944, she was damaged by two bomb hits at Leyte Gulf. On 7 April 1945, *Yamato* was sunk by US carrier aircraft 130 miles southwest of Kagoshima with the loss of 2498 lives.

SPECIFICATIONS

COUNTRY OF ORIGIN: Japan
CREW: 2500
WEIGHT: 71,110 tonnes (71,659 tons)
DIMENSIONS: 263m x 36.9m x 10.3m (862ft 10in x 121ft 1in x 33ft 10in)
RANGE: 13,340km (7200nm) at 16 knots
ARMOUR: 408mm (16.1in) belt, 231–200mm (9.1–7.9in) deck, 546mm (21.5in) on barbettes, 650–193mm (25.6–7.6in) on main turrets
ARMAMENT: 9 x 460mm (18.1in), 12 x 155mm (6.1in), 12 x 127mm (5in) guns
POWERPLANT: quadruple-screw turbines
PERFORMANCE: 27 knots

Zuikaku

Zuikaku and her sister, *Shokaku*, were the most successful carriers operated by the Japanese Navy. They were considerably larger than previous purpose-built carriers, and were better armed, better protected and carried more aircraft. The wooden flight deck was 240m (787ft) long and 29m (95ft) wide, and was serviced by three lifts. *Zuikaku* formed part of the carrier task force whose aircraft attacked the US Pacific Fleet base at Pearl Harbor in December 1941, and subsequently participated in every notable fleet action of the Pacific war: Java, Ceylon, the Coral Sea, the Eastern Solomons, Santa Cruz, the Philippine Sea and Leyte Gulf. Her name means Lucky Crane and her sister ship was *Shokaku* (Happy Crane), sunk in June 1944 by the US submarine *Cavalla*. *Zuikaku* was sunk in action by American forces on 25 October 1944, during the Battle of Cape Engano in Leyte Gulf.

SPECIFICATIONS

COUNTRY OF ORIGIN: Japan
CREW: 1660
WEIGHT: 32,618 tonnes (32,105 tons)
DIMENSIONS: 257m x 29m x 8.8m (843ft 2in x 95ft 2in x 29ft)
RANGE: 17,974km (9700nm) at 18 knots
ARMOUR: 45mm (1.8in) belt, 162.5 (6.5in) over magazines, 97.5mm (3.9in) on flight deck
ARMAMENT: 16 x 127mm (5in) guns
POWERPLANT: quadruple-screw turbines
PERFORMANCE: 34.2 knots

Index

WEAPONS OF WAR